PENNSYLVANIA'S
Black History

BY CHARLES L. BLOCKSON
EDITED BY LOUISE D. STONE

PORTFOLIO ASSOCIATES • INC.
Philadelphia, Pennsylvania
1975

Acknowledgements

This book became a reality through
the efforts of the following people:

Art Director; Lisa Werchow
Photographer; Suzan Oristaglio
Graphic Assistant; Diane Edwards

Published by Portfolio Associates, Inc.

Library of Congress Cataloging in Publication Data
E185.93.P41B56   974.8'004'96073   [B]   75-39135

Manufactured in the United States of America

To Noelle

and all black women
who made our yesterdays
possible, our present exciting,
and who provide us
with hope for tomorrow.

2500 copies of this publication are being distributed by the Pennsylvania Conference of N.A.A.C.P. Branches as part of the Bicentennial Human Rights Congresses, 1976.

CONTENTS

Contents

PREFACE

Many years ago I began collecting material on and by black people in this country and in particular the state of Pennsylvania. This book is a product of those years of research and travel. It is also a result of an unquenchable desire to see recorded the history of black people, one almost totally neglected by historians, and made available to others who also value the achievements of blacks. It is perhaps more difficult to research the black presence because blacks came to these shores not as people and individuals but as property. Record keeping was a precarious activity among people who lacked writing skills. In some counties, particularly the northern counties, there is little evidence available describing black life. In part, this is due to the extremely small black population percentages. I take full responsibility for unintended omissions or factual errors.

It probably will be impossible to pay tribute to all who have helped to make this book possible. I'm indebted to the many historical societies and libraries for the cooperation they have given in obtaining access to published materials. All praise and thanks to Dr. Dorothy Porter, who recently retired as librarian of the Moorland and Spingarn Afro-American Collection at Howard University; her counsel and encouragement were invaluable assets. I wish to express my thanks to Maxwell Whiteman for his interest in the manuscript and to my fellow members of the Pennsylvania Abolition Society for their generous grant. I am indebted to my family who, through their interest in my work, gave unknowing inspiration. Finally, I would like to give a special thanks to Dr. James E. Mooney, Director of the Historical Society of Pennsylvania, for his invaluable editorial judgment and his consistently intelligent aid in helping me organize this material.

I hope that this book stimulates others in the search (which is not an easy one) for information surrounding the black presence, especially the deeds of black women.

C.L.B. 1975

INTRODUCTION

This book reflects a journey undertaken to bring from obscurity the missing links in the history of our commonwealth—the black history. It was a journey to many counties and towns; to the newspaper files, letters, books and diaries in whose pages I found some materials that I knew existed and others that I stumbled across by happy accident.

From the research, two prominent facts emerged. First, that there was great diversity in the people and the roles they played in our history. And secondly, that the exploitation of black people by the dominant society was so sustained that a major theme of black life has been the struggle for freedom from oppression.

While the English settlers who came to Pennsylvania identified with William Penn's dream of a free society, the guarantees of liberty they formulated were limited to white men. Peaceful relations with the Indians, a feature of early colonial life, did not last; white settlers pushed farther and farther west, claiming as their own the territories they entered. By the time of the Declaration of Independence the Indians had yielded most of their land in Pennsylvania. Perhaps it was the shared experience of exploitation that led to the interaction of blacks and Indians here as in other states. Indians gave refuge to runaway slaves, often adopting them into tribal life and frequently intermarrying.

Prior to the Civil War the antislavery cause was of paramount importance. Pennsylvania became a key state in the activities of the Underground Railroad, a loosely organized system of escape routes for fugitive slaves. Many homes in Pennsylvania served as "stations," or places of hiding where fugitives were sheltered for a short time before being taken to the next stopping place. The owner of the home was known as a "station keeper" or "conductor" for he might also take the fugitives or "passengers" to the next station on the line. Agents sometimes worked in antislavery offices, providing contact from one station to another by numerous secret devices and sometimes they went directly to slaves to get them started on their northward journey. While many writers give credit to the whites who assisted fugitive slaves, it was black people who began the Underground Railroad and who were most often found to be assisting other blacks. Cooperation between the races was essential for the cause of abolition to succeed.

In a sense, the lives of black Pennsylvanians took on a dual character. On the one hand, forced exclusion from the mainstream brought about the creation of separate institutions and lifestyles. On the other hand, black residents never ceased their efforts to change the dominant white society. While blacks built their own schools they also demonstrated, withheld tax money, and spoke out againt the segregation that denied their children entrance to the public schools. When an amendment to the state constitution in 1838 barred black men from the ballot boxes they began a thirty-year struggle for the restoration of their voting rights. When the Thirteenth, Fourteenth and Fifteenth Amendments granted freedom, voting rights and citizenship, the struggle in some ways intensified. The black struggle for justice continues with unabated fervor.

The paragraphs that follow indicate, in a sweeping fashion, that black Pennsylvanians have been and continue to be pioneers and authorities in the Arts, Politics, Social Service, Medicine and Sports.

THE ARTS

From the earliest days of the Commonwealth to the present time, black Americans made invaluable contributions to Pennsylvania's cultural life and to life beyond its borders.

Negro slaves, brought to this country, were mostly inhabitants of West Africa where the arts had developed into a high degree of sophistication. Some of the qualities that served to refine the arts survived the trip to the colonies and provided America with its unique folk music and dance. Through poetry, songs, spiritual and secular, slaves and freemen expressed, subtly and not so subtly, sorrow and secrets. It was not until the Revolutionary War that craftsmen began to make substantial inroads into the various branches of the fine arts and crafts. Silhouette makers, portrait painters, carpenters, blacksmiths, silversmiths and furniture craftsmen were among the colonial blacks who were motivated by pride of good workmanship and necessity.

In the early years several black artists gained prominence. Robert M. Douglass, Jr., was born in 1809 of a West Indian father and Grace Bustill Douglass, the daughter of Revolutionary War hero Cyrus Bustill. Robert Douglass, Jr., was noted for his sign, ornamental, and portrait painting and lithography. His two famous works are portraits of President Fabré Geffard of Haiti and Frank Johnson, a conductor of the Philadelphia Orchestra. Other black portrait painters included David Bustill Bowser, a cousin of Robert Douglass: Bowser's most outstanding work is a portrait of Abraham Lincoln. The son of a well-known Philadelphia caterer, William H. Dorsey painted portraits, as did John P. Burr. Grafton Tyler Brown, born in 1841 in Harrisburg achieved recognition also.

More famous names included Horace Pippin, Henry Tanner, sculptors; Edmonia Lewis, Meta Vaux Warrick and May Howard Jackson. Allen Freelon, painter, poet and musician, came along after 1895. Rex Gorleigh of Penllyn, Laura Waring (from Hartford, but closely associated with Pennsylvania), Thaddeus G. Moseley, Elvise Bishop, Henry P. Jones, Humbert L. Howard, Paul Keen, Jr., Charlotte White Franklin, Selma Burke (designer of the Franklin Roosevelt dime), portrait painter Charles C. Dawson, and turn of the century portrait painter, Edward Stidum are well-known names in art discussions.

Trained in Dusseldorf, Germany, John Chaplin was an artist who lived and worked in Huntingdon County during the last three quarters of the nineteenth century. His paintings, done mostly on cardboard and wood, have recently been discovered and recognized as a significant historical legacy.

Other Pennsylvanians known for achievements in fine arts and commercial art are: James S. Brantley, Elmer Brown, Barbara Chase Riboud, Reginald Gammon, Russell Gordon, Jerry Pinkney, Ramound Saunders, Anna Sawyer, Charles Searles, Paul Waters, Roland Ayers, Lillian Dorsey and Aubry Panky.

Young artists active in the Philadelphia area are: Moe A. Brooker, James Gadson, Michael Kendall, Garnetta L. Lovett, Richard Watson, Pheoris West, Clarence Wood and Barkley Hendriks. Philadelphia was and continues to be, a center of art and culture attracting individuals to its many schools, museums and places of historical significance.

MUSIC & THE PERFORMING ARTS

Folk music like folk literature became a separate body of expression by the middle years of the 1800s. Some was derived from Africa, a large part was developed in America and especially in the southern part of the country. Much of the music was a result of a group effort and transmitted orally. Before Emancipation, ragtime music sprouted up along the rivers, in river towns and on the eastern coast of America. Pennsylvania had its share of popular piano players.

Walter Gould, known as "the one-leg Shadow," was a noted eastern ragtime player who played and wrote rags before Scott Joplin's *Maple Leaf* rag was published. He was born in Philadelphia in 1875 and derived his name from the wooden leg that supported him.

Charles Luckeyeth Roberts played ragtime for society's upper crust, Main Line Philadelphians and New Yorkers—during the 1920s. His childhood was spent in Philadelphia. He wrote music for fourteen musical comedies.

Over the years, blacks from Pennsylvania have supplied the nation with many outstanding entertainers. Songwriter Harry T. Burleigh came from Erie, and composer James A. Bland, although a New Yorker by birth, spent many years in Philadelphia and is buried in Lower Merion. William Raymond of Lock Haven and Ethel Waters of Chester, both singers had occasion to work together on stage.

It is difficult enough for serious white composers and musicians to get a hearing in this country—it was and still is almost impossible for serious black composers and musicians, but singer Marian Anderson and conductor James DePriest managed to pioneer in that discipline. Samuel L. Evans, the first black impresario and concert manager of the Academy of Music and founder of the American Foundation for Negro Affairs has received acclaim.

In dance circles, choreographer and dancer Arthur Hall is an established Pennsylvania name. He is Director of the Ile Ife Black Humanitarian Center in Philadelphia which is the home of Arthur Hall's Afro-American Dance Ensemble. Dance suggests the name Judith Jamison, star of the world famous Alvin Ailey Dance Group.

Dance also conjures up *Harlem's Dancingest Man*, Bill Bailey—Bill "Bojangles" Robinson's hand-picked successor. Bill Bailey, who has spent most of his years calling Philadelphia home, is the brother of Pearl Bailey.

Represented among today's popular entertainers are individuals who grew up in Philadelphia—Bill Cosby, Chubby Checkers (Ernest Evans), singer-dancer Lola Falana and gospel singer Marion Williams.

The list of jazz musicians is long and top heavy with pacesetters. From Philadelphia there are such artists as: Philly Joe Jones, Grover Washington, Beryl Booker, Ray Bryant, Joe Carroll, Bill Doggett, Jimmy Heath, Percy Heath (b. North Carolina), Charles Wright Johnson, Tommy Potter, Rex Stewart, Harry Alexander White, Elmer Gibson and Norman Connors.

Jimmy Smith of Norristown won international fame on the jazz organ.

From Pittsburgh there is: Art Blakey, Ray Brown, Paul Chambers, Kenny Clarke, Billy Eckstine, Roy Eldridge, Erroll Garner, Ahmad Jamal, Mary Lou Williams and Joe Williams.

Earl Hines (Duquesne, Pa.), Maxine Sullivan (Homestead, Pa.), the Mills Brothers (Bellefonte, Pa.), are musicians from other regions in Pennsylvania.

Innovator and saxophone wizard John Coltrane, although born in North Carolina, is associated with Philadelphia. Nina Simone, who attended Philadelphia's Curtis Institute, is typical of artists who were attracted to Philadelphia schools but who were not natives.

The "Philadelphia Sound", a unique blend of rich, sophisticated, "people" music is the creation of Philadelphia song writers and producers, Kenneth Gamble and Leon Huff.

The first recorded evidence of black actors appears in the 1760s. A black character, named Mungo, appeared in the play, *The Padlock.* An unnamed black actor played a minor role in Murdock's *Triumph of Love* at the Chestnut Theatre in Philadelphia in 1776. Murdock introduced the character *Sambo* to the American stage.

Theatre traditions are carried on by playwrights Ed Bullins, Bill Gunn, and Leslie Lee, director and physician Bill Lathan and set designer Bill Howell.

The Colored Players Film Corporation of Philadelphia produced *Ten Nights in a Barroom*, (1926), *Children of Fate*, (1927), and *Scar of Shame*, (1928). Few survived the infant black film industry.

Freedom Theatre, housed in the basement quarters of Heritage House, is the oldest and most prominent black theatre in the Delaware Valley. Its entrance is located on the Master Street side of the building. Freedom Theatre was created in 1966 as the cultural segment of the Black People's Unity Movement and originally located at the Church of the Advocate in North Philadelphia. Freedom Theatre is open year-round with a school for young people, one for adults and scheduled play performances. Its prominence is largely owed to John Allen, Jr. and Robert Leslie.

LITERATURE

As early as the 1700s black literary and debating societies sprang up in Philadelphia and Pittsburgh.

Until very recently, it was thought that the first novel published by an American black woman was written by Frances Ellen Watkins. That distinction belongs to Emma Dunham Kelley, author of *Megda* (1891). The mistake occurred when a bibliographer misdated the Kelley work. Very few copies of the first edition have been located.

Philadelphia long reigned as the capital of black letters. The Black Opals, a literary group which flourished during the 1920s, received encouragement from Dr. Alain E. Locke, a Phi Beta Kappa graduate from the University of Pennsylvania. The list of literary figures included Jessie Fauset, a novelist, and her brother Arthur Fauset, who wrote *Black Gods of the Metropolis*. In addition to the contemporary novelist, Kristin Hunter, other recognized Philadelphia writers are Angelina Grimke, Leslie Pinkey Hill, William Gardner Smith, David Bradley, Dr. Ira DeA. Reid, author, sociologist and former professor at Haverford College, John Wideman, Pittsburgh Rhodes Scholar, author, professor, and athlete, and Jean Toomer of Doylestown, Bucks County.

POLITICS & THE STRUGGLE FOR SOCIAL JUSTICE

Two black newspapers have figured in the political arenas of black and white worlds. The Philadelphia *Tribune* is the oldest, continuous publishing black newspaper in the United States, established in 1884 by Christopher J. Perry. Perhaps better known throughout the nation is the *Pittsburgh Courier*, established in 1907. Its editor, Robert Lee Vann, served as a member of Franklin Roosevelt's black Cabinet and was the namesake of a World War II battleship.

It is commonly thought that conventions of blacks focusing on black political activities are a phenomenon of the nineteen-sixties and years close to that decade. The first free black political convention was organized in 1831 in Bethel Church (or what is now called Mother Bethel Church) in Philadelphia. The convention met annually for the next five years paving the way for state conventions held by blacks shortly after the Civil War. A Negro convention held in 1848 urged Negroes to abandon the word "colored" and especially the words "Africa" and "African." Philadelphia leaders recommended use of the phrase "Oppressed Americans."

Separatism was a central theme to the pre-Civil War conventions. In 1830 black emigration to Canada was encouraged at the Convention of the American Society of Free Persons of Color. At the second Convention of Colored People held in Philadelphia in 1832, the idea of Canadian colonization met with objections. At other conventions emigration to Africa, Haiti, and South America was vigorously argued which proves that present day notions of separatism are reaffirmations of pioneer black thoughts.

The first black woman legislator in the state was Crystal Byrd Fauset, who won a seat in the House of Representatives in 1938. Judge Juanita Kidd Stout was the first black female judge in Pennsylvania. The first black elected to a Common Pleas Court judgeship was Raymond Pace Alexander of Philadelphia. His wife, Sadie Tanner Alexander, also an attorney, received the first Ph.D. awarded a black woman in economics at the University of Pennsylvania. She is the first black woman to graduate from the University of Pennsylvania's Law School. Both she and Raymond Alexander worked actively in human rights fields.

William H. Hastie, a Federal Judge of the Third Circuit Court was the first black man to receive such an appointment. He was also the first black Governor of the Virgin Islands. His younger colleague, A. Leon Higginbotham, Jr. was appointed United States District Judge for the Eastern Region of Pennsylvania in 1963. Robert N.C. Nix, Jr., was the first black man to be named to a seat on the State Supreme Court. His father is a U.S. Congressman from Philadelphia. Other "firsts" in Pennsylvania state government include K. Leroy Irvis, State Representative and the first black House Majority Leader. C. DeLores Tucker of Philadelphia is the state's first black Secretary of State. Finally, in the wider political world, William T. Coleman is the second black man to hold a Secretaryship on the federal cabinet level, and the first black man to be Secretary of Transportation, serving in the Ford administration. Coleman has been President of the N.A.A.C.P. Legal Defense Fund and was the first black admitted to the Union League. Reverend Leon Sullivan created his now nationally known O.I.C. in Philadelphia (Opportunities Industrialization Centers).

MEDICINE

Pennsylvania blacks who made history in the field of medicine include the noted physician, Charles Burleigh Purvis born in Philadelphia and the son of the wealthy abolitionist, Robert Purvis, graduated from Western Reserve University in Ohio in 1864.

Among the black Pennsylvania physicians who founded hospitals were Dr. Nathan F. Mossell the first black to graduate from the University of Pennsylvania Medical School. Dr. Mossell founded the Frederick Douglass Memorial Hospital in Philadelphia in 1895. Dr. Henry M. Minton founded the Mercy Hospital in 1907; the two hospitals later merged and became known as the Mercy-Douglass Hospital, in 1948. Dr. Frank Boston founded the North Penn Hospital in Lansdale, Montgomery County in 1934. Dr. John Q. McDougald and Dr. Helen O. Dickens of Philadelphia won national recognition in medicine.

SPORTS

Black Pennsylvanians have achieved state, national, and international recognition in athletics as amateurs and professionals. They have participated in virtually every major sports competition on field, court, and track.

The Pythians baseball club, thought to be the first black team in the United States, was formally organized in Philadelphia in 1867. That same year the newly formed National Association For Baseball players, also in Philadelphia, passed a resolution barring the participation of black clubs. Although the Pythians were the first organized black baseball team, blacks may have participated in the game well before the Civil War, for it was known as a popular pastime in this country after 1839.

The first black man playing on an otherwise all-white team in Pennsylvania was Bud Fowler, reportedly playing second base with the Newcastle team in 1872. In the late nineteenth century and early twentieth century, most black players took part in all-black clubs. The Homestead Grays of the old Negro league, starred Josh Gibson, who was said to have been the greatest right-hand hitter of all time. In Darby, the Darby Daisies, owned by businessman John M. Drew, began as a sandlot team and went on to delight fans all along the eastern seaboard.

After the Second World War, black baseball players from Pennsylvania played with predominantly white teams. Numbering among the best known players are Roy Campanella from Philadelphia, who played with the Brooklyn Dodgers; Richie Allen from Wampum, of the Phillies; Reggie Jackson from Wyncote, with the Oakland Athletics; and David Rickets from Pottstown, who played the position of catcher in the National League. (His brother, Richard, a pitcher, also played professionally.)

Blacks played football on college teams in Pennsylvania since the early days of this century. Among those who went on to national fame are: Dan Tyler of Donora; Wallace Triplett of La Mott and Dennis Hoggard of Philadelphia; both played for Penn State in the 1948 Cotton Bowl, where they were the first black players to compete there. Lennie Moore of Reading starred at Penn State and won fame with the Baltimore Colts. Herb Adderly of Philadelphia went to Michigan State and played with the Green Bay Packers. Sandy Stevens of Uniontown played at the University of Minnesota and in the professional leagues of Canada. Emlen Tunnell of Garrett Hill became an all-time defensive halfback with the New York Giants, and was the first black football player inducted into the Hall of Fame. The first black captain of the University of Pennsylvania's football team was Robert Evans. His teammate, Edward Bell, became the first black to make All-American from the University of Pennsylvania. James Nance from Indiana, Pennsylvania started as fullback at Syracuse University and went on to play with the Boston Patriots. Billy Joe of Coatesville starred at Villanova and with the Denver Broncos.

Among the famous black basketball players from Pennsylvania are Chuck Cooper of Duquesne; Maurice Stokes of St. Francis; Wilt Chamberlain, Guy Rodgers, Walter Hazzard, and Frank Washington, all of Philadelphia—Washington starred with the Harlem Globetrotters.

In boxing, two black Philadelphians hold world championship titles, Robert Montgomery, lightweight champion, and Howard Johnson, light heavyweight champion. Former world heavy weight champion Joe Frazier, a native of South Carolina, lives in Whitemarsh, Montgomery County.

Blacks have been setting and breaking track and field records in Universities and during their participation in numerous World Olympics. The noted Pennsylvania athletes are:

John B. Taylor	University of Pennsylvania, 1908 Olympic winner—1600 meter relay team.
Benjamin Johnson	Plymouth, Pennsylvania sprinting record breaker—Columbia University.
John Woodruff	Connelsville and University of Pittsburgh, 1936 Olympic first place—800 meter run.
Herbert Douglass	University of Pittsburgh, 1948 Olympic medal winner.
Arnie Sowell	Pittsburgh and University of Pittsburgh, 440 and 880 meter intercollegiate record setter, 1956 Olympic team.
Norwood (Barney) Ewell	Lancaster, 1948 Olympic 100 and 200 meter dash, 400 meter relay team.
Roderick Perry and Arthur Pollard	Coatesville and Penn State University, sprints and hurdle record setters.
Joshua Culbreath	Norristown and Morgan State College, 1956 Olympics—400 yard hurdles world record breaker.

Robert Barksdale	Norristown and Morgan State College, former world's indoor highjump record.
Irv Robeson	Philadelphia and Cornell University, 1960 Olympics—broadjump.
Bruce Collins	Chester and University of Pennsylvania, 400 meter intercollegiate hurdles record setter.

Only one black female Pennsylvanian stands out in athletics, Ora Washington of Philadelphia, who was talented in several fields, during the 1920s and 1930s. While she has participated in track, golf and basketball, she is best known as a tennis player. Angel Doyle recently has won international fame in track and field as a high school student from Harrisburg.

BUCKS

AND

MONTGOMERY
COUNTIES

Bucks County and Montgomery County are immediate neighbors north of Philadelphia. Rich in history, they have been home for generations of blacks and the stage of early antislavery activity. Washington Crossing State Park is the scene of an annual reenactment of General Washington crossing the Delaware on Christmas Day. Moravians who settled around the Doylestown area brought pottery skills and today tile and pottery industries cluster there.

PLACES

BUCKINGHAM: MOUNT GILEAD CHURCH   *BUCKS*

Last Stop on Underground Railroad

Up a winding path, hidden in a grove of trees, there still stands Mount Gilead Methodist Church, the last main stop on the Underground Railroad in Pennsylvania. From this point in Bucks County, fugitive slaves were transported across the Delaware River into New Jersey.

Built of logs in 1835, the original church was situated on Buckingham Mountain a few miles from New Hope, Pennsylvania, on Holicong Road, in Buckingham.

An escaped slave, called Big Ben, served as the church's first minister at the religious services, sometimes known at that time as camp-meetings. He is buried in the little cemetery in front of the church.

Today, church services are held only twice a year—a sunrise service on Easter Sunday and a Memorial Day Service in May.

EDGE HILL   *MONTGOMERY*

Law Circumvented—Blacks Own Land

The village that came into existence where Limekiln Pike passes over Edge Hill near Cheltenham Township was known as Guineatown. The land was initially conveyed to Richard Morrey (or Maury) from his Huguenot father in 1715. After freeing his father's slaves, he leased one hundred acres legally to Mrs. Mounteer who, as a black woman, could not own property. In May, 1838, the people of Guineatown held a meeting and decided to change the name of the area to Edge Hill Village. They inscribed the new name, placed it on top of a May pole, and celebrated the joyous occasion. There remains, of old time Guineatown, only a small burial ground of 75 graves from the slave family who took the name of their former master. A Knights of Columbus building is located today on the grave site and a street sign bearing the name of Mounteer accompanies it in what is now known as Glenside, Pennsylvania.

Cremona Morrey, another slave who took her master's name, received an additional 198 acres from Richard Morrey in 1772. To circumvent the question of black ownership the tract was deeded to her husband John Frey, a freed man, who adopted his master's name. Frey and five other free blacks, placed the land in trust to Isaac Knight of Abington, thereby maintaining the right to sell the tract for 30 shillings. When the land was again sold after the Revolutionary War, several impressive estates were established on this ground: Twickenham, the first home of Thomas Wharton, president of the Supreme Executive Council of Pennsylvania was among them. Another estate built on the former Morrey land, Gray Towers, is now part of Beaver College.

Woodlawn: Father Divine's Estate

Thousands filled streets, churches and halls to see and hear the words of inspiration from one of the most fascinating religious figures of the century. George Baker, known to millions as Father Divine, along with other such heavenly titles as the "Prince of Peace," the "Everlasting Father," and "Mighty God," attached both white and black followers to his flock.

Divine was a brilliant organizer and businessman. His material kingdom has been estimated at more than six million dollars. His conviction and his motto, "Father will provide," resulted in his being called one of the most successful sociological phenomena of his time. His wealthy estate, Woodlawn, is found in the hilly section of Gladwyne, Pa. The Divine Lorraine Hotel, on North Broad Street in Philadelphia, and the Divine Tracy in West Philadelphia are properties of Father Divine's real estate holdings. A son of a former slave, he died in Philadelphia in 1965.

11,000 Blacks Trained for Civil War

Camp William Penn, where 11,000 black soldiers were trained for service in the Civil War, was once located in the community called LaMott. On July 17, 1862, Congress enacted a bill authorizing the President "to employ as many persons of African descent as he may deem necessary and proper for suppression of the rebellion." On January 1, 1863, the President signed the Emancipation Proclamation relating to the slaves held in the disloyal states and the federal government leased a portion of Oak Farm, extending from Old York Road to Penrose Avenue and from City Line to Beech Avenue as a training camp for black soldiers. The site was called Camp William Penn. The town itself was originally called "Camptown," however, in 1885 the name was changed to honor Lucretia

Mott who lived in the vicinity of the former campsite. The first recruits arrived at Camp William Penn on July 4, 1863. The camp then became the first recruiting and training center for black soldiers to be operated by the United States government. General Louis Wagner was chosen commandant of the camp.

Today a historical marker honors this former Civil War campsite which once was composed of long rows of frame barracks, mess halls, guard houses, officers' quarters, and a chapel. The camp was also self-contained to prevent the black troops from entering Philadelphia which was a few miles away. Such were the anti-military prejudices of the day.

LANGHORNE: GUINEA RUN   *BUCKS*

Freed Slaves Settle Near Langhorne

During the early days of slavery in Pennsylvania it was not uncommon for slaves to receive provisions for a new life as well as their freedom. Judge Langhorne, the person for whom the small historic community is named, freed his own slaves in his will on October 11, 1742. The group consisted of thirty or forty slaves on his plantation, Langhorne Park, on the main road from Bristol in Bucks County. The older blacks remained on the premises; to six others he gave land to own or lease and in addition, horses and cows, sheep, farming tools, and household goods, while each of the younger slaves was to receive ten pounds when he or she became twenty-four years old. Several of the houses were situated near a small stream which flowed into the Neshaminy Creek. The settlement was called Guinea Run.

Wedgwood's Antislavery Medallion: 1788

The Buten Museum of Wedgwood, exhibits one of the original medallions commemorating the founding of the London Society for the Abolition of Slavery in 1788. The colorful medallion, of basalt and jasper, shows a slave in chains, kneeling and with hands outstretched imploringly, and the inscription "Am I not a man and a brother?"

The medallion was first struck by Josiah Wedgwood, a wealthy English potter and abolitionist. Wedgwood sent a number of these plaques to Benjamin Franklin, then President of the Pennsylvania Abolition Society, for distribution among Society members. During the height of the abolitionist movement several decades later, a new, smaller coin modelled after Wedgwood's medallion was produced for sale at the antislavery fairs. As the fairs were organized mainly by women, a similar coin representing the oppressed slave woman was struck with the inscription: "Am I not a woman and a sister?"

The Buten Museum lies in Lower Merion Township, just beyond the Philadelphia boundary.

African and Black American Art

With an early interest in Negro art, Albert Barnes under the guidance of his friend, Dr. Alain Locke, a Philadelphian and Rhodes Scholar, built a collection of African art and creations of black Americans. Specifically, he was impressed with primitive painter Horace Pippin, a native of West Chester, Pennsylvania. Barnes was a physician/chemist who made a fortune manufacturing a popular pharmaceutical product. He invested a fortune in Impressionistic art work which is housed in his beautiful home, now a museum, on Latches Lane in Merion, Pennsylvania. The collection, one of the finest in the world, is open to the public on a restricted basis.

NEW GOSHENHOPPEN   *MONTGOMERY*

Lawyer Fights For Slave Family

This small Pennsylvania Dutch village was the center of controversy following the death of Rev. George Michael Weiss, the pioneer minister of the Reformed Church of Goshenhoppen, near East Greenville. Weiss, a slave owner, left no will upon his death, and his property, including land in Greenlane and a family of slaves, passed to his widow. The widow died in 1765, and bequeathed her property to the resident black family of slaves. When the slave family sought to take possession of the parsonage of the New Goshenhoppen church, the church officials resisted declaring that the house and land were the property of the congregation and that the minister and his family lived there by permission of the congregation, and that neither Weiss nor his wife could dispose of the estate by will. Aid came to the slave family from Israel Pemberton, the Quaker philanthropist of Philadelphia who was concerned for the rights of blacks and Indians. Pemberton felt that the slave family of Goshenhoppen was entitled to the Weiss property and he engaged prominent lawyers to fight the slave family's battle in court. The available records do not show the outcome; however, the New Goshenhoppen church is still standing today and has apparently survived the curious sequel to the death of the Rev. George Weiss.

NORRISTOWN, FIRST BAPTIST CHURCH   *MONTGOMERY*

Former Slaves Address White Congregation

In Norristown, the First Baptist Church once located on the corner of Airy and Swede Streets, and its pastor, Rev. Samuel Aaron, actively supported antislavery causes. Many persons in the white congregation assisted in the Underground Railroad and Aaron, an eloquent orator himself, often invited abolitionist leaders to speak from the pulpit in support of antislavery ideas and activities. Such noted abolitionists as William Lloyd Garrison, Wendell Phillips, Frederick Douglass, and Lucretia Mott were among the speakers to address the congregation. Former slaves who had safely traveled the route to freedom also appeared at the church to give accounts of their perilous journeys. Among them was Henry "Box" Brown who, having found a hiding place in a box measuring only two by three by three-and-one-half feet, survived a twenty-six hour transport from Richmond, Virginia to Philadelphia in a box which had been mistakenly turned upside down.

Henry "Box" Brown

Despite Rev. Aaron's great efforts, the congregation was divided over the antislavery issue. Some members remained in favor of slavery and would heckle Lucretia Mott at a meeting for appearing on the arm of black abolitionist Frederick Douglass. Civil War General Winfred S. Hancock and his family left the congregation because of its involvement in antislavery activities.

Segregated Monument to Civil War Soldiers

In the tree-lined public square next to the County Courthouse between Main and Airy Streets in Norristown, there stands a marble bronze monument with the following inscriptions: *"Erected by the citizens of Montgomery County, September 17, 1869. In honor of our brave soldiers and sailors who fell while defending the Union during the great Rebellion, A. D. 1861-1865."* Separated from the names of their white comrades on the rear lower portion of the monument is a section dedicated to the United States Colored Troops, honoring the following who gave their all for their nation:

E. Willmore, Sergeant	*William VanLeer, 127th Regiment*
Robert Brown, 8th Regiment	*James Wilson, 137th Regiment*
Embrose Jackson, 41st Regiment	*Isaac Hopkins and George Price,*
Daniel Davis, 45th Regiment	*54th Massachusetts Volunteers*

Sergeant Albanus Fisher of Norristown who survived the conflict served with the 54th Regiment.

PLYMOUTH MEETING   *MONTGOMERY*

Abolition Hall

Abolition Hall in Plymouth Meeting, Pa. was built by George
Corson of the noted Quaker and abolitionist family of
Plymouth Meeting. This hall, which comfortably accommodated one hundred fifty to two hundred persons, also served as
a station on the Underground Railroad. The Hall later served
as a studio for the noted American painter, Thomas Hovenden.

Also located in this historic village is the house where
Thomas Hovenden painted his well-known view of the slave's
friend, John Brown, who gave his life for the abolition of slavery. Hovenden's painting is housed in the Metropolitan
Museum of Art. It portrays Brown leaving the Courthouse on
his way to his execution. Hovenden married into the notorious
abolitionist Corson family who fought for the rights of slaves
and women. The Corson house is located at the intersection of
Spring Mill Road and Butler Pike.

VALLEY FORGE   *MONTGOMERY*

Black Soldiers, Seamen, Spies, and Slaves

Positioned in two counties off of the Pennsylvania Turnpike
on State Route 23 (Interchange 24), is Valley Forge Park, site
of General Washington's encampment. Historians have recorded the bravery of many white Revolutionary War heroes;
however, until recently, the deeds of the black soldiers who
endured the cold winter of 1777-1778 had been overlooked.
Although the first martyr of the American Revolution, Crispus
Attucks, died in Boston on March 5, 1770 protesting against
oppression, it is estimated that of the three hundred thousand
soldiers who served in the Continental forces, five thousand
were black. Billy Lee, for example, served Washington faithfully as the general's personal slave, and was constantly with
him. Cyrus Bustill, a black baker from Philadelphia, brought
bread to Valley Forge for the starving armies. In like manner,
Salem Poor, the hero of Bunker Hill, shared the bitter cold
here with his comrades. Phillip Field, another black patriot of
the 2nd New York Regiment, died here in 1778. Rev. Richard
Allen, one of the most respected black men of his day, brought
salt and supplies from Rehoboth, Delaware to Washington's
troops at Valley Forge.

Black soldiers were fighting side by side with their white
comrades in most units of the Continental Army by the sum-

mer of 1778. Hardly a ship sailed in the Continental Navy without a black gunner, officer's helper or seaman.

Custer, a black shipwright from the Southwark section of Philadelphia, served in the navy during the war. He participated in a raid on Tory pirates near Billingsport in 1778 where he cut off the head of one of the pirates. He brought this grisly trophy back to Philadelphia and proudly placed it on display in a Sansom Street tavern where the head attracted much attention.

Pompey, a black slave belonging to General Lamb, rendered invaluable service as a spy at Stony Point, New York, on July 16, 1779. He also contributed to the victory of the Continental forces under General "Mad Anthony" Wayne, for

whom Wayne, Delaware County, Pennsylvania, is named, being acclaimed a hero for his brilliant military tactics against the British soldiers.

In an old white stone house, the former home of slaveowner Isaac Potts, General George Washington had his headquarters from Christmas Day, December 25th, 1777, to June 19th, 1778. The Montgomery County town of Pottstown honors the name of Potts.

Throughout the historic and hallowed campsites at Valley Forge are monuments honoring the heroic fallen soldiers who fought under General Washington and his aide, General Lafayette. However, there is no visual evidence of those courageous black patriots who participated in the bitter fight for independence in this area. Yet it is recorded that Lafayette praised the 144 black troops who fought with him and under the leadership of General Nathaniel Greene.

Lafayette asked Washington, at one time, to join him in a plan to free the blacks. The following letter was written by Lafayette from France on February 5th, 1783:

"*Now, my dear General, that you are going to enjoy
some ease and quiet, permit me to propose a plan to
you which might become greatly beneficial to the
black part of mankind. Let us unite in purchasing a
small estate, where we may try the experiment to free
Negroes, and use them only as tenants. Such an example as yours might render it a general practice; and if
we succeed in America, I will cheerfully devote a part
of my time to render the method fashionable in the
West Indies. If it be a wild scheme, I had rather be
mad in this way, than to be thought wise in the other
task.*"

Washington replied to Lafayette on April 5th, 1783:

"*The scheme, my dear Marquis, which you propose
as a precedent to encourage the emancipation of the
black people in this country from that state of bondage in which they are held is a striking evidence of the
benevolence of your heart. I shall be happy to join you
in so laudable a work; but will defer going into a
detail of the business till I have the pleasure of seeing
you.*"

The plan never became a reality. Many of the black patriots
who fought for liberty from British rule and for freedom from
tyranny were once again compelled to serve under the squalid
and sordid institution of slavery.

Lafayette praised James Armistead, a slave from New Kent
County, Virginia, who served under him. Armistead was
perhaps the most celebrated master spy of the Revolutionary
War, serving both the British and Continental armies.
Lafayette wrote of Armistead that the black spy "properly acquitted himself with some important communication I gave
him," and that "his intelligence from the enemy's camp were
industriously collected and more faithfully delivered." Armistead respected Lafayette so highly that he changed his name
to James Armistead Lafayette in honor of the French general.

When the British General Cornwallis surrendered and was
visiting at Lafayette's headquarters, it is recorded that
Cornwallis "was amazed to see the black slave" he believed to
be his own clever spy for the British, playing a dual role.

Earlier, General James M. Varnum, a young and confident
soldier was head of the court martial section in the Continental forces while they were encamped at Valley Forge. He was
sent to Rhode Island to recruit black men for service. During
this period a black company of pioneers was organized under

Captain Allen Stewart from Philadelphia, in 1777-1778, to fight in the war for independence from Great Britain.

The historic Memorial Chapel located at Valley Forge pays glowing tribute to such foreign generals as Lafayette, Von Steuben, and Kosciuszko, but leaves the black trooper unmentioned.

The home of Mr. and Mrs. F. Woodson Hancock, located on Valley Forge Road, was once a famous station on the Underground Railroad. During the days of slavery, many fugitive slaves seeking freedom were led to this home then owned by a leading Pennsylvania antislavery and Underground Railroad agent, Elijah Pennypacker. Along with Lewis Peart, Pennypacker hid hundreds of slaves in the Valley Forge vicinity while they were on their way to freedom in Canada.

WASHINGTON'S CROSSING   *BUCKS*

Prince Whipple Oarsman With Washington

A marker commemorating the brave deeds performed by the soldiers of the Continental Army who crossed the Delaware River on that cold wintry Christmas Day in 1776 is located at Washington Crossing State Park. Among Washington's troops were many blacks; two well known names were Oliver Cromwell (who lived to be a hundred), and Prince Whipple, the bodyguard to General Whipple of New Hampshire. Prince Whipple, the black oarsman who was with Washington in the small rowboat, gained fame through the well-known engraving depicting the crossing by artist Emanuel Gottlieb Leutze in 1851. Whipple (front of boat) has been portrayed as a white figure in other historic renderings of this event.

PEOPLE

Alice of Dunk's Ferry   *BUCKS*

Although little is known of this curious figure, Alice, she is included on these pages because she lived so long that she became an oral historian, a memory source for those whose lives shared the same time span.

In 1686 Alice was born in Philadelphia of slave parents who had been brought from Barbados. She lived in Philadelphia until the age of ten. A slave master then moved her to Dunk's Ferry, seventeen miles up the Delaware River in Bucks County. This remarkable woman, who vividly recalled the founder of the state, William Penn, and who survived the first president of the United States, George Washington, died at the age of 116 years in Bristol, Pennsylvania.

Alice collected tolls at Dunk's Ferry bridge. She is remembered on horseback galloping to Christ Church at the age of ninety-five years.

When returning to Philadelphia, Alice frequently would describe to those who would listen, the original wooden structure of her beloved Christ Church. She was so well respected that she is included with such others as Joan of Arc and Empress Catherine I of Russia in a book of biographical sketches, *Eccentric Biography; or Memoirs of Remarkable Female Characters, Ancient and Modern,* published in 1803 by Isaiah Thomas.

James A. Bland   *MONTGOMERY*

Over 600 songs, including *Carry Me Back To Old Virginny,* official state song of Virginia, *Oh, Dem Golden Slippers,* theme song of the Philadelphia Mummers, and *"In The Evening By The Moonlight,"* are attributed to James A. Bland, black minstrel comedian and composer. After poverty and toil in beer gardens and clubs in the city of Washington, D.C., in the 1870s, Bland's fame spread over America and to Europe during the 1890s. He retired to Philadelphia where he lived lonely and penniless. Upon his death there was no money for even a modest funeral or grave marker. An overdue tribute to Bland by a Howard University graduate and son of one of the very first black college graduates in the country, came as late as July, 1941.

Governor William M. Tuck and the Lions Club of Virginia accorded Bland an honorary burial in the Merion Cemetery, Bala Cynwyd, Pa.

Sung with Great Success by Alma Gluck

Carry me Back to Old Virginny
Song and Chorus
by
James A. Bland
50
Boston-Oliver Ditson Company
NewYork-Chas.H.Ditson & Co. Chicago-Lyon & Healy

Edward (Ned) Hector   MONTGOMERY

Hector was a black patriot of the Revolutionary War who served in the Battle of Brandywine in September, 1777. As a private in Captain Hercules Courtney's Company, Third Pennsylvania Artillery Continental Line, he saved the day for the American forces. He died in 1834, at the age of 90 and the following obituary which appeared in two Norristown newspapers recalled his heroism and saved Hector's name from obscurity:

> "*Edward Hector, a colored man and a veteran of the Revolution. Obscurity in life and oblivion in death is too often the lot of the worthy. They pass away, and no 'storied stone' perpetuates the remembrance of their noble actions... During the War of the Revolution, his conduct, on one memorable occasion, exhibited an example of patriotism and bravery which deserves to be recorded. At the Battle of Brandywine he had charge of the ammunition wagon attached to Col. Proctor's regiment and when the American army was obliged to retreat, an order was given ... to abandon the wagons to the enemy. The heroic reply of the deceased was uttered in the spirit of the revolution: 'The enemy shall not have my team. I will save the horses, or perish myself!' He instantly started on his way, and as he proceeded, amid the confusion of the surrounding scene, he calmly gathered up ... arms which had been left on the field by retreating soldiers, and safely retired with wagon, team, and all in the face of the victorious foe. Some years ago a few benevolent individuals endeavored to procure him a pension, but without success. The Legislature of Pennsylvania, however, at the last session granted him a donation of $40.00—which was all the gratuity he ever received for his Revolutionary service.*"

Hector's grave lies in Upper Merion Township. His cabin was located on the southwest corner of a street in Conshohocken which today bears his name, Hector street.

One of Hector's contemporaries, John Francis, another black soldier from Pennsylvania, lost both legs in the Battle of Brandywine. Francis served under Captain Eppel and Colonel Craig, and he was pensioned out of service on May 21, 1787.

Efforts are now under way to procure a marker to commemorate Edward (Ned) Hector by the Conshohocken Historical Society.

Hector's daughter-in-law, Leah, is buried in an unmarked grave in the cemetery of Christ Church, Swedesburg, Upper Merion Township. She was a former slave who died at the age of 107 on March 4, 1887. An account at the time of her death said "she was an amazing woman who, for the past 100 years, prepared her own kindling wood. She was tall, gaunt and double jointed. Her mind was sharp and could recall many events in United States history, particularly the time she saw General George Washington. She remembered that her mistress paid $3,000 for her." At the time of her death Leah Hector was a resident of the Montgomery County Alms House.

Benjamin Lay MONTGOMERY

In 1737 Benjamin Franklin published *All Slavekeepers That Keep the Innocent in Bondage, Apostates Pretending to Lay Claim to the Pure and Holy Christian Religion,* written by an eccentric, hunchbacked, tiny Quaker vegetarian named Benjamin Lay. He wrote this work to denounce the evils of slave holding, often dramatizing his views by fasting for months at a time.

In 1735, this former slave trader arrived from the West Indian Island of Barbados. While a resident of Abington, he wrote a 271 page book giving explosive testimony against this "filthy leprosy" (slavery) destructive to religion and government. He was known for dramatic incidents. In one meeting, he took a sword and ran it through his coat. When he removed it the blade was soaked with blood (it had punctured a filled bag concealed beneath his clothes). He shouted, "Thus shall God shed the blood of those persons who enslave their fellow creatures."

Lay, who lived to be over eighty years of age, added needed fuel to the antislavery cause and paved the way for other less dramatic workers in the antislavery movement.

Lucretia Mott

Lucretia Mott   MONTGOMERY

Only a gatehouse remains to mark the existence of *Roadside*, a major station on the Underground Railroad and formerly the home of abolitionist Railroad agents, James and Lucretia Mott. As a suffragette and representative to the 1859 World Anti-Slavery Conference in London, Mrs. Mott was among the noted Americans who supported the cause of freedom in this country. Small in stature and weighing only ninety pounds, she was often called by writers of her day the Black Man's Goddess.

The Motts' *Roadside* home saw persons dedicated to the abolitionist movement as constant guests; famous and obscure, American and foreign, men and women. Among them were William Lloyd Garrison, Frederick Douglass, John Greenleaf Whittier, British abolitionist actress Frances Kemble, and the slave liberator John Brown who was hanged at Harper's Ferry. Lucretia Coffin Mott who died November 11, 1880, is buried in Friends Fairhill Cemetery on Germantown Avenue at Clearfield Street, Philadelphia.

Stiffany   MONTGOMERY

A county newspaper in September 1777 carried this report on a runaway "handy" female slave:

Twenty Dollars Reward

"Ran away from the subscriber. Living in Whitpain township, on the 26th of September, 1777, a mulatto wench Stiffany, about 26 years old, middle sized, active, handy wench; had on and took with her a black bonnet, a calico long gown, four striped linen and linsy short gowns, five linsy petticoats, three shifts, two yards and a half of home made linen, one or two pairs of shoes and sundry other wearing apparel. She likewise stole and took with her a black horse with a star in his forehead, short thick neck, his mane declining to hang on both sides of his neck. Whoever apprehend and procures said wench, so that her master may get her and the horse, shall have a reward—16 dollars for the wench and 4 for the horse, and reasonable charges paid by

James Knox"

CHESTER
AND
DELAWARE
COUNTIES

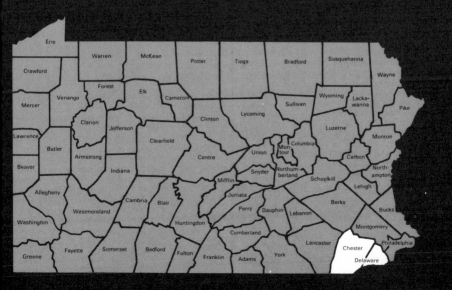

These most settled and oldest counties have seen their character change radically in the centuries since their settlement. Once rural, with small town centers, they have become heavily urbanized along the major auto routes and along the Delaware River. Oil refineries, factories, shipyards and other industrial complexes have long attracted blacks looking for employment.

Other parts of the counties are crisscrossed with farmland; some noted for the production of mushrooms.

Before 1850, there were very few blacks in Radnor, a locality in Delaware County. Radnor contained fewer slaves than surrounding townships because living was harder, farmland not as fertile and Quakers were in abundance. In 1780 legislative action required that slaveowners register the names of their slaves lest the slaves receive immediate freedom, no one took this action in Radnor. Assessment in the year 1783 indicated that there were only five blacks in a total population of 524. Radnor's first black landowners were Charles Humphrey's servants, Tome and Judy.

The antislavery movement was very unpopular along the Main Line. Thus the meetings of antislavery societies were very secret. In 1837 the Wilberforce Antislavery Society was founded by the residents of Berwyn and Wayne. In 1838 the Wilberforce Antislavery Society joined with other antislavery groups such as those in Gulph, East Fallowfield and the Chester County Antislavery Society in a general resolution denouncing all slave labor or "the fruits thereof." The Society's "togetherness" dwindled as the years approached 1850. The spirit of those involved moved "underground" for safety sake. The present Billy Walker Farm located on the north side of U.S. 202 and east (½ mile) of King of Prussia was, before and during the Civil War, a famous Underground Railroad station. Formerly it was part of the estate of Senator Jonathan Roberts who was an enthusiastic supporter of emancipation and equal rights for blacks.

PLACES

CHESTER (CITY)   *DELAWARE*

Underground Railroad Route

Swedish settlers founded Chester, the oldest city in Pennsylvania, in 1644. They named it "Uppland" and William Penn renamed it Chester in honor of one of his English companions.

On March 5, 1857, Chester, situated strategically on the route of escaping slaves, was the scene of a bloody battle between twelve blacks fleeing slavery and ten slave catchers. The fugitives turned on their pursuers and fought until the slave catchers beat a hasty retreat. The blacks escaped, aided by abolitionists from nearby Philadelphia, into Knowles Pines forest.

Chester is also remembered as the birthplace of the well-known blues singer, dancer and actress, Ethel Waters, who came to personify the *Charleston* dance in the 1920s and whose singing won her the title of *Sweet Mama Stringbean.*

For a brief time Reverend Martin Luther King lived in Chester where he attended Crozier Theological Seminary.

COATESVILLE   *CHESTER*

A Shocking Incident

A shocking and violent event took place on August 14, 1911, in Coatesville, a small Chester County community. A black named Zachariah Walker was accused of murdering Edgar Rice, a special police officer who was employed at the Worth Iron Mills. After being discovered hiding in a tree, Walker shot himself in the mouth, but he failed to kill himself as intended. He was later taken to a hospital for treatment. Hearing the news that a police officer was killed, an angry mob of white citizens attacked the hospital, smashing doors and windows. After gaining entrance to the room where Walker was resting on a cot, the mob carried him through the streets of the town to a local farm. The masked crowd tied Walker to a cot and built a fire. As the flames grew, Walker's ropes burned through, and he ran for freedom. However, he was seized again and dragged back to the fire where he met his death. The fragments of Walker's charred bones, all that was left of his body after his fiery death, were distributed among the crowd as souvenirs.

For years many map makers were embarrassed by this shameful incident and they deleted the name of the town of Coatesville from various maps of Pennsylvania.

Downingtown Industrial and Agricultural School

Founded in 1905 by the Rev. Dr. William A. Creditt, Downingtown Industrial and Agricultural School provided industrial and manual training for black students. Its largest building, Pennsylvania Hall, was erected entirely by black mechanics. A predominantly black teaching staff offers a highly specialized industrial course to its students. It once served as a preparatory school for Lincoln University in Oxford.

Honoring Black Controlled Nation

This small predominantly black village is located near Coatesville. It was originally settled by fugitive slaves, who named their community after the West Indies island of Haiti. This black controlled nation's heroic leaders were three former ex-slaves, Toussaint L'Ouverture, Jean Jacques Dessaline and Henri Christophe. Christophe used guerrilla tactics to defeat the greatest expeditionary army ever assembled in the West Indies—the elite of Napoleon Bonaparte's forces of over 35,000 men.

Lincoln University

Founded in 1854 by a group of black Presbyterian ministers, among whom was John M. Dickey, who served as a missionary preaching to slaves in Georgia. Ashmun Institute, as Lincoln was originally named, was established to provide education for black male youths. During the days of the Underground Railroad, the chapel on Lincoln's tree-lined campus served as a hiding place for runaway slaves. Lincoln has produced distinguished black alumni in a variety of fields, among them Langston Hughes whose private collection of books is housed in the Vail Memorial Library at the University.

Lincoln is situated near the border of Lancaster County, near Route 1, in Oxford, Pennsylvania. This oldest black college boasts of graduates such as: Thurgood Marshall, Associate Justice of the Supreme Court; Rev. James Robinson, founder of Operations Crossroads; Kwame Nkrumah, Chief of State of Ghana; Nnambi Azikiwe, Governor General of Nigeria; and Horace Mann Bond, educator, author and father of Julian Bond.

PHOENIXVILLE   *CHESTER*

Schuylkill Friends Meeting House

Located in Phoenixville, one of the chief towns in Chester County, the Schuylkill Friends Meeting House served as a station on the Underground Railroad and as a place where noted antislavery speakers could air their views. John Greenleaf Whittier was among that group. Some blacks are buried in the cemetery behind the Meeting House, which is still in use.

SHARON HILL   *DELAWARE*

Queen Of The Blues

North of Chester, Mt. Lawn Cemetery, in Sharon Hill, holds the grave of Bessie Smith, queen of the blues singers and perhaps the most famous of all blues singers. Her discovery was owed to Ma Rainey, another legendary blues singer, who persuaded her to join the Rabbit Foot Minstrel group after hearing her sing in Chattanooga, Tennessee.

Bessie Smith died of injuries from an auto accident. She was refused admission to a hospital in Memphis near the scene of the accident. Her body was shipped north. Bessie Smith was married to Jack Gee, a Philadelphia policeman.

For many years the grave site was unknown. Mrs. Barbara Muldow, a black housewife brought the matter to the attention of the *Philadelphia Inquirer* and the late singer Janis Joplin provided a tombstone for the neglected grave.

WEST CHESTER *CHESTER*

Cheyney State Teachers College

Chester County is the home of two black academic institutions, Cheyney State College, founded in 1837 by Philadelphia Quakers, and Lincoln University. Cheyney was formerly the Institute for Colored Youth and was established to prepare blacks for teaching. Its wooded campus is accessible from Route 1.

Notable Cheyney graduates include: former School Superintendent (Oakland, Calif.) Marcus Foster, Crystal Byrd Fauset, the first black woman ever elected to the Pennsylvania State Legislature; and Rebecca Cole, the first black woman admitted to medical school in the United States.

PEOPLE

Pennock Barton *DELAWARE*

Pennock Barton, a black seaman from the suburban Philadelphia township of Darby in Delaware County, sailed on the *True Yankee* in 1813 as a gunner. He manned the long gun when it captured the British East Indian *Boadicea* in the Indian Ocean. Barton's captain had offered him fifty guineas and the best suit of clothes on the captured ship if he would bring down the topmast. The prize brought 100,000 pounds. Barton won his fifty guineas, his share of the prize money, and a British major general's uniform.

Horace Pippin *CHESTER*

Horace Pippin, a black artist noted for his primitive paintings, was born in West Chester in 1888. Pippin never received a formal art education though he drew and painted from an early age. While serving overseas in World War I he was severely wounded and partially paralyzed. He continued painting and achieved recognition during the 1930s. Two of his most important paintings are *John Brown Goes to His Hanging* and *Buffalo Hunt*. His paintings today are found in the collections of the Barnes Foundation of Merion, and Whitney Museum of Art in New York City, and many others.

Ethel Waters *CHESTER*

Married at age twelve, Ethel Waters worked as a maid in Philadelphia hotels and later in a similar capacity at Swarthmore College. After landing a singing job at the Lincoln Theatre in Baltimore, she worked the second string club scene until she substituted for the famous Florence Mills in New York City's *Plantation Club,* in 1923, and created a sensation. Her stage roles were in *Blackbirds, Rhapsody in Black, As Thousands Cheer,* and *Home Abroad.* Film roles included *Cabin in the Sky* and *Pinky.* She is remembered for the Broadway production of *The Member of the Wedding* in 1950. Television performances have since rounded out her theater career. Her book, co-authored with Charles Samuels in 1951, is called *His Eye is on the Sparrow.*

CENTRAL REGION

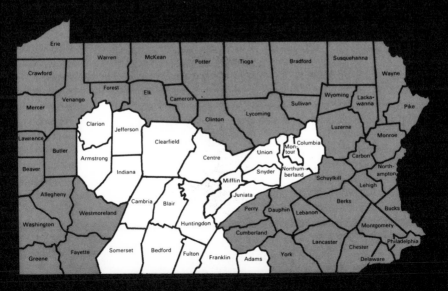

A terrain of great diversity with heavy forests, cleared pastures and mountain ranges, running southwest to northeast, characterizes the central part of Pennsylvania. A number of cities of varying sizes have attracted blacks to their industries which include tanning and allied trades, light manufacturing and coal mining. The two rivers dissecting this area are the Susquehanna and the Cumberland.

Blair County, referred to as the gateway to the Alleghenies, is situated in an area of caves and caverns noted for their scenic beauty. Pennsylvania's largest remaining virgin timber stands in Cook Forest State Park in Clarion County.

Somerset, Bedford, Fulton, Franklin and Adams Counties border the state of Maryland and are of a mixed economy which includes heavily wooded areas, farmland and scattered small towns. There are few black families in this area with the exception of a large colony at Chambersburg attracted by light industry. The region is probably best known for Gettysburg, the site of a decisive battle of the Civil War. The town offers many museums and also contains the room where President Lincoln is reputed to have put the finishing touches on his famous address in 1863. Gettysburg is also the location of one of Pennsylvania's two national parks, Gettysburg National Military Park, where history is recreated in many forms for the thousands of yearly visitors.

After the Civil War, Johnstown, an area in Cambria County, received its first black residents—Joseph Allen, Andrew Mallatt, Jacob Crowley, Charles Cook, William Roberts, Louis Rideout and their families. The Woodvale Tannery was their invitation to employment. Johnstown is the chief commercial center of Cambria County, originally settled in 1769. This county figured prominently in doing its share of aiding runaway slaves—legal authorities generally refused to assist marshals and slave owners. Many of the runaway slaves entered Cambria County by way of Bedford which was the most favored station.

In Mifflin County, on February 18, 1861 blacks in Lewistown held a meeting at the home of John L. Griffith to consider migrating to the West Indian island of Haiti. As a result, seventy people left Lewistown, with a small group from Bellefonte. Of the remaining blacks, the *Lewistown Gazette* reported, in February and March of 1861, that several fought in the Civil War, for the Union, representing Lewistown. In 1912 Richard R. Wright wrote in his *The Negro in Pennsylvania: A Study in Economic History,* that blacks in Lewistown owned property and businesses.

PLACES

Heroes Of Bellefonte

Due to the strong antislavery influence in Bellefonte among the Quakers, many of the fugitive slaves from the southern states, after reaching Centre County, settled in Bellefonte prior to the Civil War. St. Paul's Church, organized in 1859, served a black population of several hundred shortly after emancipation. Black men, representing Bellefonte as well as several other sections of Centre County, gave evidence of their loyalty to the Union by rendering their services in the Civil War.

Two other blacks from Centre County served in the Civil War with honor; Wesley Miller and Samuel Henderson, a former agent on the Underground Railroad. An underground newspaper on the campus of Penn State University in that county is named for Henderson who fought for dignity and justice for his race. He, along with a number of white citizens in Centre County, were avowed abolitionists. The first known abolitionist was William H. Robinson, who said, "May the swarthy sons of Africa be free as the white population in the United States and slavery no longer stain the annals of our history."

The *History of Centre County, Pennsylvania* lists the following names of blacks who were members of the Sixth Regiment, United States Colored Soldiers, in Companies F and G, August 26, 1863 to September 20, 1865:

> *Delige, Alexander, Patton*
> *Delige, Hartsock, Patton; died at Wilmington, N.C., Aug. 3, 1865*
> *Derry, William, Bellefonte; killed at Petersburg, July 8, 1864*
> *Green, William, Bellefonte; disch. Sept. 20, 1865*
> *Johnston, Washington, Bellefonte; disch. July 12, 1865*
> *Johnston, Moses, Bellefonte; drowned in James River, Aug. 29, 1864*
> *Lee, Benjamin, Bellefonte*
> *Lee, Charles, Snow Shoe; corp: disch. Sept. 20, 1865*
> *Miles, Lewis, Bellefonte; disch. Sept. 20, 1865*
> *Whitten, John W., Bellefonte*
> *Whitten, John, Patton*
> *Worley, Aaron C., Bellefonte*

John W. Whitten was a private in Company K, 8th Pennsylvania Regiment, United States Colored Troops. Captured in early 1865 by the Confederate Army, he was later sold by the Confederates into slavery in Cuba. Whitten escaped in 1889 and returned home to Bellefonte. He served as a prisoner of war for twenty-four years, a record unequalled by any other American soldier. Sarah Whitten Stoner, his mother, is buried in the small Methodist Cemetery at the Centre County town of Pleasant Gap.

Another venerable black citizen of Bellefonte was William H. Mills, who had operated the town's oldest barber shop until his death on July 17, 1931. He was born in Bellefonte in 1847 and was the foremost member of St. Paul's A.M.E. Church, where he was an ordained minister. In 1909, Mills published a history of the church from the time of its founding. In his younger days, Mills was recognized as a singer and together with other local persons he formed a concert company which played engagements in many parts of Bellefonte and adjoining counties. His relatives, the world renowned Mills Brothers, sang and carried this family tradition of music around the world.

BLOOMSBURG *COLUMBIA*

Black Elected To Town Government: 1872

The one "first" for a small black community in Bloomsburg was the election of James Dennis to the town's government seat in 1872. A small group of fugitive slaves escaping from the south settled in Bloomsburg prior to the Civil War and established the A.M.E. Church which still stands. However, today it is used by members of a Pentecostal sect.

CASSELMAN *SOMERSET*

Negro Mountain

A short distance from the small town of Casselman are two mountains—Mt. Davis, the highest point in Pennsylvania, and Negro Mountain. The last mountain was so named, according to tradition, in honor of a slave in Captain Andrew Friend's party who came to Somerset County from Maryland in 1755 in order to explore the mountain region's rich reserves of deer, elk, wild turkey, panthers, bears, and other game. The Indians who inhabited the area had served notice to the white men not to enter the game territory and the slave, said to have been of gigantic stature, very strong and armed, was mortally wounded by them. Captain Friend and his party fought their way back to him and, though he pleaded for their hasty retreat without him, they stayed until his death and buried him among the roots of a fallen tree. Friend and his party returned safely to Fort Cumberland. The name of Negro Mountain is still found on maps of Pennsylvania.

CHAMBERSBURG *FRANKLIN*

John Brown's Headquarters

On King Street, just east of Second Street, in Chambersburg, stands the two-and-a-half story house of the notorious abolitionist John Brown. He was an expert in guerilla warfare, and had fought a fierce and bloody battle in Kansas against the proslavery forces. Brown was the leader of a small, well-disciplined group of antislavery fighters. He became nationally known as "Old Brown of Osawatomie." His ambition was to liberate the slaves held in captivity in the south through armed insurrections. During the summer of 1859, Brown moved quietly to Chambersburg describing himself as a prosecutor under the name of Isaac Smith. At his headquarters he received large boxes of weapons marked tools and shared with no one his plans to raid Harper's Ferry (now West Virginia) with a small band of followers, several of whom were his sons. The raid on the federal arsenal failed. Brown, thinking there would be an immediate revolt by slaves was disappointed when there was no reaction. Brown and his men were trapped after capturing the arsenal; however, two days later thirteen of Brown's men including two of his sons had been killed. Only a

John Brown

Jessie Glasgow

41

few escaped. Brown was captured by a company of United States Marines under the command of Colonel Robert E. Lee. He was later tried and hanged on December 2, 1859.

The last words of John Brown were on a slip of paper, written the morning of his execution. On his way out of the jail he handed it to a guard at the door. It read as follows:

Charlestown Jail
December 2, 1859

"I, John Brown, am now quite certain that the crimes of this guilty land will never be washed away except with blood. I had, as I now think, vainly flattered myself that without much bloodshed it might be done."

His sincerity stimulated the North to sympathy towards the antislavery movement. Those citizens who once mocked and harassed the abolitionists at the beginning, a few years later, during the Civil War, marched as Union Soldiers into battle singing the stirring words, "John Brown's body lies a-mouldering in the grave, but his soul goes marching on." Black people of today still remember with reverence this brave white martyr. A brilliant black scholar, W. E. B. DuBois, wrote that John Brown did more to shake the foundation of slavery than any single person in America. The life and times of John Brown has served as a subject of fascination for years by many writers. Jessie Ewing Glasgow, a bright young student of the University of Edinburgh, published a pamphlet in 1860 entitled *The Harper Ferry Insurrection.* He was one of the first blacks to interpret the impact of Brown's raid. Glasgow was a member of the first graduating class of the Institution for Colored Youth, now called Cheyney State College.

GETTYSBURG   *ADAMS*

Colonel's Report Hails Black Soldiers

Black soldiers saved the day for the Union Army of Abraham Lincoln at the Battle of Columbia Bridge.

One of the Confederate generals, Robert E. Lee, who planned the invasion of Pennsylvania, was halted heroically by a company of black soldiers hailing from Columbia, Lancaster County, on Sunday, June 28, 1863, after three white companies from Columbia had returned to their homes.

The black men valiantly took up their arms and held their ground; destroying the Columbia Bridge structure by fire. This prevented the Confederate forces from crossing the Susquehanna River—making a glorious victory!

A record of this historic episode can be found in a vivid account by the author of *Memorial of Patriotism of Schuylkill County, Pennsylvania*—Colonel G. Frick, the commanding officer of the integrated company of soldiers, who wrote:

> *"Before closing this report, justice compels me to make mention of the excellent conduct of the company of Negroes from Columbia. After working industriously in the riflle-pits all day, when the firing commenced, they took their guns and stood up to their work bravely. They fell back only when ordered to do so."*

There once was a small black community in what is now Adams County. Although the community had its own churches, cemeteries, and schools, it left few traces in the form of artifacts, records, or institutions. It is recorded that blacks participated in the Battle of Gettysburg as cooks, laborers, teamsters, and servants. However, a group also saw action in the actual battle. After the authorization of enlistment by Lincoln, blacks fought and died in many of the remaining battles of the Civil War.

The mill of Colonel McAllister, located during the period of slavery, on Rock Creek, between Cumberland and Mt. Joy Township, was a station of the Underground Railroad. The Doblin House in Gettysburg is alleged to have been a station on the Railroad, and currently the museum in the building shows a black mannequin in the hiding place under the steps. The black mannequin represents Gettysburg and Adams County's participation in the Underground Railroad system.

Black Civil War Soldier

LEWISBURG   *UNION*

Underground Railroad Commemorative Marker

On University Avenue in Lewisburg, the Pennsylvania Historical and Museum Commission has erected an historical
marker with the following information:

Underground Railroad

*This old stable was a station on the Underground
Railroad. Here fugitive slaves were hidden, fed and
aided in reaching the next station on their journey.*

MERCERSBURG: MASON-DIXON LINE   *FRANKLIN*

Africa In Mercersburg

Mercersburg, a small and densely wooded Franklin County
community close to the Mason-Dixon line, served as a haven
for fugitive slaves during the era of the Underground Railroad.
Slaves would often travel from the slave state of Maryland
over the narrow passes of the Cove Mountains. Though the
final destination of these courageous blacks was Canada and
freedom, many established small communities in the Mercersburg area. One of these communities was known as Africa,
consisting of twenty-five families.

WILMORE   *CAMBRIA*

Black Founds And Settles Town

A quiet and scenic little town, Wilmore in Cambria County
was founded and settled by Godfrey Wilmore, a black man and
native of Baltimore, Maryland, shortly after the Revolutionary
War. He migrated to the frontiers of Pennsylvania with his
white wife and built a home about one-half mile south of what
is now Wilmore Borough. The site-name honors the family,
despite the town government's proposal insisting on
Guineatown and Jefferson as desirable names. In 1832 a post
office was opened and carried the name Wilmore, which exists
until this day. While Cambria County is not a border county on
the Maryland line, its neighbor to the south, Bedford County,
led slaves into Cambria County. Thus Cambria County became a haven for runaway slaves coming from the South.

PEOPLE

William Whipper

Born in the home of a white Columbia lumber dealer where his mother served as a maid, William Whipper became one of the nation's first black capitalists. Whipper and another black man, Stephen Smith, were partners in a lumber business. They owned extensive coal and lumber property and railroad boxcars in Columbia, Norristown and Philadelphia.

A noted abolitionist, Whipper used his home as a station on the Underground Railroad in Pennsylvania. Fugitives came to York and then crossed the Susquehanna River at Wrightville. The long bridge from Wrightville to Columbia was the only safe outlet after 1847. Revealing his participation in the operation of the railroad Whipper wrote:

> *"My house was at the end of the bridge, and as I kept the station, I was frequently called up in the night to take charge of the passengers.... On their arrival they were generally penniless and hungry. I have received hundreds in that condition; fed and sheltered from one to seventeen at a time in a single night. Some went to Pittsburgh by boat, others 'in our cars' to Philadelphia. Until the passage of the Fugitive Slave Law in 1850, many remained in Columbia to work in the lumber and coal yards."*

The Fugitive Slave Law made the penalties for aiding the escape of slaves more severe than ever before. Oddly, this seemed to have the opposite effect intended. Northerners, involved in the cause of freedom, refused to be intimidated by this legal threat and passed Personal Liberty Laws. Southerners resolved to take full advantage of the Fugitive Slave Law. Obviously, hostilities increased on both sides.

An incident occurring in Columbia illustrates the results of such legislation, passed without regard for human life. William Smith, an escaped slave long before 1850, lived in Columbia and was respected as a useful member of the community. One day while at work he noticed an approaching band of men. Suspecting that they might be slave catchers and frightened at the prospect of being returned to his former master, Smith began to run. In the hunters' effort to catch him, Smith was fatally shot.

Dr. Daniel Hale Williams   *BLAIR*

Daniel Hale Williams was a black surgeon who, in 1893, performed the first open-heart surgery in history on a young street fighter suffering from a knife wound in Chicago, Illinois. Dr. Williams founded the first interracial hospital in America, Provident Hospital in Chicago. President Grover Cleveland appointed Dr. Williams surgeon-in-chief of Freedman's Hospital in Washington, D.C. Later he was elected a Charter Fellow of the American College of Surgeons. He returned to Chicago to be the first black at St. Luke Hospital and Northwestern University Hospital.

Daniel Hale Williams' father, representing Hollidaysburg, was one of the seventy-one who met at the Harrisburg State Equal Rights Convention of the Colored People of Pennsylvania in 1865.

At the age of twelve in Hollidaysburg, Daniel Williams was working as an apprentice shoemaker and at seventeen he was a barber. He drifted to Illinois where he met a white physician who encouraged him to enter medicine. At the time he opened a practice in 1883, no black physicians were allowed to use any hospital facilities in Chicago so he opened Provident Hospital.

Bedford Springs was the birthplace of George Washington Williams. The fountains of mineral water that still flow steadily from the ground, were used medically by the Indians in the area and their alleged healing qualities were passed on to the early settlers. Before the Civil War, wealthy southerners travelled long distances to bathe in the springs, around which grew a health resort.

In 1849 George Washington Williams was born of African, German, and Welsh ancestry. After having nearly completed his studies at Newton Theological Seminary in Massachusetts when the Civil War broke out, Williams volunteered in the Union Army enlisting under the name of his uncle. Due to his intelligence and education he fared well in the army, entering as a private and leaving in 1865, when the war ended, as a sergeant major.

Williams rejoined the army in Texas and fought against Maximilian in Mexico. During this time he advanced to the rank of lieutenant colonel.

From 1868 to 1874 he resumed his studies in various theological seminaries. Beginning with a career as a Baptist minister, he went on to find fame as a newspaper reporter, federal clerk in Washington, lawyer, Judge Advocate of the Grand Army of the Republic, novelist, poet, traveller, and magnetic orator. However, it is as a historian that he accomplished his most valuable work when he wrote the classic two-volume *History of the Negro Race in America from 1619 to 1880* which was published in 1883. Williams researched the book for seven years. The work began with "Kingdoms of Africa" and ended with the "Exodus."

He states his reason for writing the book at the end of the second volume:

> *"Race prejudice is bound to give way before the potent influences of character, education, and wealth and these are necessary to the growth of the race. Without wealth there can be no leisure, without leisure there can be no thought, and without thought there can be no progress. The future work of the Negro is two-fold; subjective and objective years will be devoted to his education and improvement in America. He will sound the depth of education, accumulate wealth, and then turn his attention to the civilizations of Africa."*

Williams' monumental work received favorable and lengthy reviews in several major American and English magazines. Six years later Williams presented his publishers with another well-documented text: *A History of the Negro Troops in the War of Rebellion, 1861-1865.*

George Washington Williams died at the age of forty-two years.

CAPITAL AREA

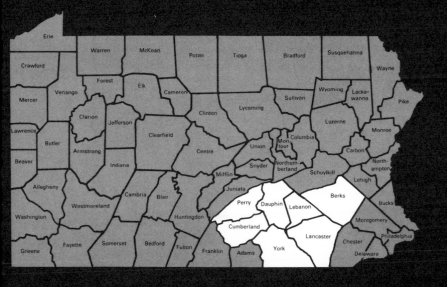

Sometimes referred to as the Capital area, this region contains Harrisburg, the state capital and political focus of eleven million Pennsylvanians. The magnificent 475 room Capitol is the dominant building of the group of ten in Harrisburg. The Susquehanna River travels through these counties and cuts across the state capital, providing one component for industries which dot the river valley towns. South of the area and west of the Susquehanna is York in the county of the same name—a town that was at one time considered for the capital of the United States.

The Great Appalachian Valley in Pennsylvania is represented by the twenty mile wide Cumberland and Lebanon Valleys.

The region west of the more densely populated southeastern counties includes one of the richest agricultural areas in the state. Lancaster is the heart of Pennsylvania Dutch country—Amish, Dunkard and Mennonite lands, Hershey chocolate and tobacco production.

Blacks here were slaves of various ethnic masters, but the Amish and Mennonite families did not favor the use of slaves. Consequently the antislavery sentiment pervading this region's atmosphere led to a sense of confidence and security among those blacks who called this area home.

The town of Steelton, outside of Harrisburg, has had a large black population since Civil War times.

PLACES

BALLY: ST. PAUL'S CATHOLIC CHURCH   *BERKS*

Pension Stolen From Revolutionary War Veteran

Founded as a parish in 1741, by the Jesuit priest, Reverend Theodore Schneider, St. Paul's Catholic Church was built in 1743. The name was changed to The Most Blessed Sacrament, in 1827. The original name of the small village of Bally was Goshenhoppen, an Indian name meaning "meeting place." It was later changed to Bally, honoring one of the church's early priests.

In the cemetery behind the church there is the grave of Isaac Jones, a former black slave who served under General George Washington. According to the church records, Jones was baptized and received the sacraments of the Catholic Church on December 23, 1847.

The following account of Jones' obituary was published in the *Reading Adler,* January 4, 1848:

> *"Isaac Jones was born about the year 1754 in Africa and died December 27, 1847, at the age of ninety-four years.*
>
> *"Isaac Jones saw service during the Revolutionary War against England in 1776, and served almost the duration of the war. After some period of service in the Continental Army, he lived for fifty years in Bucks and Montgomery Counties, earning his livelihood by sharpening knives for cutting paper, also as a wood sawer.*
>
> *"During the latter years of his life he was afflicted with great pains, finally dying on December 27, 1847, at the home of Michael and Peter Mayer, being bedfast for three months and three days. During all this time he received the very best and kindest attention.*
>
> *"After being mustered out of the Continental Army, he was entitled to receive a pension: someone for years had been drawing this pension for him but did not apply it for his benefit so he spent his last short time on earth with Michael and Peter Mayer who gave him a home."*

CARLISLE   *CUMBERLAND*

Early Fights For Freedom

Located eighteen miles west of the Susquehanna River, the Carlisle of today still possesses some of its colonial atmosphere, with shady streets camouflaging a sprawling industrial center. Dickinson College and Law School, located in this town, was founded in 1773 by Dr. Benjamin Rush, an eminent Pre-Revolutionary physician who resided in Philadelphia. He was an active friend of the cause of the oppressed blacks.

During the decades before the Civil War, the town of Carlisle was known as a notorious station stop on the Underground Railroad, harboring many fugitives fleeing from the slave-catchers. Many of those runaways were recaptured and severely punished by their masters. Early in June of 1847, an incident occurred in Carlisle that created national attention. Two Maryland slaveholders came in pursuit of three fugitives. In the fighting that followed, one of the slaveholders was severely beaten and died three weeks later. Dr. John McClintock of Dickinson College assisted the fugitives and tried to prevent their recapture. Dr. McClintock was arrested and later tried along with a number of free blacks who had participated in the sudden and violent attack. McClintock and several of the blacks who offered protection were acquitted, while the other free blacks were fined.

While living in the community, John Peck, a free black, served the blacks of Carlisle both as a barber shop owner and as an agent on the Underground Railroad. In 1837 Peck participated in the first meeting of the Pennsylvania Antislavery Society held in Harrisburg, Pennsylvania. Peck later moved to Pittsburgh, where he became an active member in several State Equal Rights Conventions of Colored People in Pennsylvania. Peck and William Nesbit of Altoona were recognized by the black communities throughout the Commonwealth as leaders. Peck, while living in Pittsburgh, also served on the Board of Trustees at the Avery College for black youth.

In 1838 a black juvenile antislavery society was formed in Carlisle, similar to those formed in several other northern cities. The society's function was to promote the abolitionist cause and to disclose the evils of slavery.

CHRISTIANA RIOT   *LANCASTER*

38 Blacks And Whites Arrested For Treason

A large monument stands on a small square in the Borough of Christiana, commemorating the historic event that took place there. The Fugitive Slave Law passed by Congress in 1850 permitted many slave catchers to "seize and arrest suspected runaways." Many freed blacks, as well as slaves, were often returned to the South and slavery. In September, 1851, a

slaveholder with his son and nephew from Maryland, encouraged by the law, and accompanied by United States marshals, traveled to Christiana after two fugitive slaves. The blacks, having received notice of their coming, gathered in a significant number at the home of William Parker, the fugitive. After an exchange of words between the two parties, shots were fired, killing Edward Gorsuch, the slave owner, and wounding his son. With the aid of antislavery people of Christiana, Parker sought asylum in the home of Dan Ross, the black Underground Railroad keeper in Norristown. The incident received national exposure as federal marshals sought Parker throughout the state. He was later forwarded safely to Canada. Thirty-eight black and white citizens from Christiana were arrested and charged with treason against the United States for violating the Fugitive Slave Law by aiding fugitives. However, a jury acquitted all of them. A detachment of forty-five United States Marines and nearly one hundred Philadelphia policemen were assigned to Christiana to restore order. Thaddeus Stevens, Congressman, abolitionist and Lancaster's most famous citizen, served as the lawyer for the defense.

HARRISBURG *DAUPHIN*

1848 State Convention Of Coloured Citizens

In 1848 on December thirteenth and fourteenth, black delegates met in the state capital of Harrisburg for the purpose of devising the most efficient method of petitioning the legislature for the elective franchise. An informal meeting was held at the Wesleyan Methodist Church of the Reverend George Gailbraith.

The delegates wrote and adopted a Constitution consisting of fourteen articles and voted to present the Constitution of Rights to the State Legislature; members of this historical convention adopted the name of "The Citizens Union of the Commonwealth of Pennsylvania."

HARRISBURG *DAUPHIN*

Pennsylvania Anti-Slavery Society

Organized at Harrisburg in 1837, the Pennsylvania Anti-Slavery Society was one of the most influential and powerful societies in the nation. By 1838 women were welcomed as active members and later several served as officers with the dedicated humanitarian Lucretia Mott, who with her husband James demanded immediate emancipation for both the slaves and women.

Two years later during the World Anti-Slavery Convention in 1840, in London, eight of the women delegates were refused seats by the Committee of the British and Foreign Society, who maintained that their admission would be contrary to British rules. Although Wendell Phillips, a leading orator of his day, made strenuous efforts to have the women seated, the Committee refused to change the rules. When the fiery Boston newspaper editor and abolitionist William Lloyd Garrison, learned that the women delegates were denied, he refused to enter the conference and took a place in the gallery as a spectator. Several other American delegates followed his example.

Dr. Julius Le Moyne of Washington County served as the Society's first President. Washington County, as early as 1782, registered a total of 443 slaves and 155 slave holders. Le Moyne represented a county which established one of the first antislavery societies in the state (1789)—the Washington Society for the Relief of Free Negroes and Others Unlawfully Held in Bondage. Among the blacks associated with the Pennsylvania Anti-Slavery Society were Robert Purvis and William Still. The society distributed about 1,500 copies of its newspaper *The Pennsylvania Freeman*.

On April 26, 1870, Philadelphia's black community held a celebration, demonstrating their joy with the adoption of the Fifteenth Amendment. A short time later on May 5, 1870, the remaining members of the Pennsylvania Anti-Slavery Society came together, declared their work done, and formally disbanded.

State Equal Rights Convention—1865

Representing 60,000 black citizens, delegates from across the state of Pennsylvania came together in the capital city of Harrisburg on February 8, 1865. The State Equal Rights Convention of the Colored People of Pennsylvania met to secure full civil rights and to restore their faith in the Union which they had valiantly fought to save.

The main issue of the Convention was an appeal to the legislature to grant the blacks of Pennsylvania the right to vote once again. The following theme taken from the minutes of the Convention expresses the mood of the delegates:

> *"We, at one time enjoyed our suffrage in this state and met but little of the cruel prejudice that now meets us at every step we make in the direction of human progress. A prejudice barring against us the doors of your public libraries, of your colleges, of your science, of your lecture rooms, of your military academies, of your jury boxes, of your ballot boxes, of your churches, of your theaters, and even your common street cars; and knowing all this to be the direct result of the defunct system of barbarism—American Slavery—we now ask that as you have slain the cause with the rebellion, you give us security against the continuance of the effect, as manifested in the existence of these inhuman prejudices and prohibitions."*

The delegates also demanded the end of the exclusion of black people from barber shops operated by those who cater to whites only and for the right of black teachers to teach black children because they understand their academic needs. The most forceful statement in the minutes read:

> *"We turn with the most pleasant emotions to that day in the history of Pennsylvania upon which the inscription upon the bell (still enshrined within the sacred temple of our liberty—Independence Hall) 'proclaim liberty throughout all the land, unto all the inhabitants thereof' will be the universal sentiment of the people of our state."*

Community Life

Among the historical Berks County landmarks, located in a green valley by French Creek, Hopewell Village today stands as a tribute to the black slave workers who invested sweat and blood into the small village two centuries ago.

It was founded in 1770 by Mark Bird, who was the largest slave owner in Berks County. The village was bustling in that time to supply cannon and shot for the Continental forces of General Washington during the Revolutionary War. Black slave workers were a part of this self-contained community during the entire history of the Furnace Operation.

Near Hopewell Village is the remains of an African Methodist Church founded by escaped slaves on their way to Canada, some of whom found work at the village furnace and foundry.

The AME Mount Frisby Church was known also as the Six Penny Colored Church and Mount Zion Church. Among the ruins at this site today are graves, some with legible names. The domestic and social life of the small community centered around the modest church building. A wall of brown field stone enclosed an area of twenty-four by thirty feet, and what was once a chimney are the remains of the church today. There is a cemetery to the south of the church site with tombstones for Isaac Cole and James Jackson, black veterans of the Civil War.

The village records have a list of terms used to describe slaves: "Man of Color," "Colored Man" and Negro. Other slaves were simply known as Black Quash, Kuba, Hester a black woman, Negro Morish, Peter Negro, Black Boy, Black Cook, or Cuff. Cuff was the name given to blacks in colonial times who didn't conform to the institution of slavery.

Hopewell Village is situated near St. Peter's Village, another picturesque old town restored as a historical site.

PINE FORGE: RUTTER'S MANOR HOUSE   **BERKS**

Quaker Dedicates Life To Racial Freedom

The manor house built in 1720 by and for Thomas Rutter became known as the Pine Forge Station, a stop in the Underground Railroad. Its cellar contained openings leading to tunnels which were used for hiding fugitives. The building above these tunnels remains a fine example of colonial architecture. The man whose energy and fortune built the home was a Quaker whose life work stood for brotherly love, racial freedom, and tolerance. It was Rutter who seconded George Keith's warning to the nation of the perils and the sin of holding and selling of slaves in the document *To Friends* printed in 1694 in Philadelphia. This protest was issued a few years after Daniel Pastorius' famous protest against slavery in 1688. Keith's document actually was printed by William Bradford and is reputed to have been the first printed warning to slave holders in America. Rutter employed slaves in his iron operation although he never owned them.

Erected on the property today are churches, dormitories, and school buildings that are operated by the Seventh Day Adventists and called Pine Forge Academy. The Seventh Day Adventists founded the Academy during the month of October, 1945, under the leadership of Elder J. H. Wagner as a religious institution whose goal was "to instill into minds the principle of Christian Character"; its student body is predominantly black.

Reading's Historical Blacks

Known as the capital of Pennsylvania's "Germanland," Reading is located on the Schuylkill River's east bank in southeastern Pennsylvania. It is a city of vastly diversified industry and commerce. With all of its historical background of German folklore, Reading offers a significant account of black history. Slaves existed in the town as early as the mid-seventeen-hundreds.

Reading and the other surrounding townships were havens for fugitive slaves. The old Kirbyville Hotel in Richmond Township was a station on the Underground Railroad with a secret attic used to conceal the courageous blacks. The Washington Street Presbyterian Church also served as a station.

Joseph Gardner represented Reading in several of the state's black political conventions, dealing with black disenfranchisement. Another convention he attended had its tenth annual meeting in Reading on August 18, 1874—the Pennsylvania State Equal Rights League.

Robert J. Nelson of this city was instrumental in the founding of the National Suffrage Convention. This organization met in Washington, D.C. in 1904 to encourage the Republican Party to argue for a stronger enforcement of the Fifteenth Amendment. Nelson was the author of the pamphlet, *Why the Colored Man Will Vote for Judge Pennypacker*. Thirty-five thousand copies were widely distributed. Pennypacker, upon being elected governor, appointed Nelson to the Commonwealth Bureau of Mines.

PEOPLE

T. Morris Chester   *DAUPHIN*

Born in Harrisburg on May 11, 1843, this tall, well built, illustrious black man distinguished himself as a writer, pamphleteer and lecturer. He was the only black correspondent to cover the Civil War and later served as Ambassador to Liberia in Africa. Chester was appointed Brigadier General of the Louisiana State Militia during the Reconstruction period.

On December 9, 1862, Chester addressed the Philadelphia Library Company of Colored Persons, emphasizing that literary contributions play an important role in the development of "self respect and racial pride." Most poignantly, he underscored "The superiority which the race has displayed under the most humiliating and disheartening circumstances," and "Arguing that the concealed facts of the past should be reproduced to vindicate our susceptibility to a higher order of excellence."

Chester charged the members of that celebrated gathering with these directives:

> *"Remove as far as all practicable, from all observations and associations, every influence which tends to weaken your self respect. Take down from your walls the pictures of George Washington and Union General George McClellan."*

> *". . . if you love to gaze upon military chieftains, let the gilded frames be graced with the immortal Toussaint, the brave Geffrard, and the chivalrous Benson, three untarnished black generals whose martial achievements are the property of history.*

> *". . . if superior intellects present any attractions, hang in the most conspicuous places the great Ward, the unrivalled Douglass and the wise Roberts, all of whom were born in the South, and under the most disadvantageous circumstances attained the highest order of statesmanship.*

> *". . . beautify your walls with scenes and landscapes connected with our history, which shall win our praise and inspire our admiration.*

> *". . . If you wish bishops to adorn your parlors, there are the practical Allen, the pathetic Payne, the*

logical Burns and the eloquent Clinton—if you want priests, there are the lamented Douglass, the gifted Garnet and the popular Schureman.

"Let your children look upon such public speakers as the brilliant Delany, the chaste Remond, the polemic Weir and the rising Catto.

"The wealth can be represented by the penetrating Smith, the economical Watson and the close calculating Whipper—the martyrs by the intrepid Green and the undaunted Copeland of Harper's Ferry Fame . . . the men of moral and holy influence by the upright Peck, the beloved Wright, and the modest Bishop . . . female excellence by the highly respected Sarah Douglass, the accomplished Joannah Howard, by the famous Aldridge and the beautiful Mrs. D'Morti—and the artists of the brush by the sanguine Bowser, the gallant Chapman and the distinguished R. Douglass.

"If you would have your children gaze upon greatness and glory, hang up the portraits of Alexander Dumas, the brilliant author; Crispus Attucks, the first martyr of the American revolution; Benjamin Banneker, the mathematician; Nat Turner, the emancipationist; Joseph Cinques, the god-like hero; Robert Small, the unrivalled strategist of the present war, and a host of others whose deeds have immortalized their names.

"The great and good men and women with beautiful associated scenes in our history, looking down from the walls, will awaken a high degree of self-respect and an exalted pride of race . . . examples for all time to come, and stimulate others to earn a place upon the scroll of fame. Impress the youths with the moral goodness and sacrificing devotion of our representatives."

With all these suggestions, Chester advised, "I would not persuade you to like the white race less, but love the black race more."

In 1881 he became the first black admitted to practice before the Pennsylvania Supreme Court. He is buried in the family plot in an unmarked grave at The Harrisburg Lincoln Cemetery.

Hercules *DAUPHIN*

Located at the foot of Washington Street in Harris Park is the grave of the founder of the state capital, Harrisburg. Harris was a fur trader from Yorkshire, England, who acquired a deed to the land which had been owned by the Penn family. Harris' son, John Harris, Jr., laid out the frontier post which later developed into a town. Prior to the purchase, the region had been owned and controlled by a group of Indians. According to local tradition, a group of drunken Indians stopped at the home of John Harris demanding an additional supply of "lum" (meaning a container of rum made in the West Indies). Upon seeing the drunken state the Indians were in, Harris refused to grant their demands. The Indians dragged him to a nearby mulberry tree with the intention of burning him to death. Harris was saved by Hercules, his black slave, who, upon hearing the cries of his master, came to his aid with a group of friendly Indians. Immediately after the heroic rescue mission, Harris freed Hercules. Many of Hercules' descendants remained in the area for years.

Thaddeus Stevens *LANCASTER*

Two of the best friends that black people have ever had were Charles Sumner and Thaddeus Stevens. Senator Charles Sumner was not a Pennsylvanian at any time and for that reason will not be discussed here, but it is necessary to mention him with Stevens as they worked and fought hand in hand for black freedom. History books treat them as a fighting pair, because they dominated the struggle for the legal foundation of equal rights. They were denounced as fanatics, burdened with loneliness and understood by few.

Thaddeus Stevens, born in Vermont, moved to Pennsylvania after 1814. He opened a law office in Gettysburg and accumulated large real estate holdings. He became involved in the iron business and at one time his iron works were destroyed by Confederate General Jubal Early. His blacksmith shop and furnace served as a station on the Underground Railroad. At Caledonia State Park in Franklin County, there is a recreation of the Thaddeus Stevens' blacksmith shop. He moved from Gettysburg to Lancaster where he accepted the cases of many fugitive slaves. When the courts ruled against his defendant he usually purchased the freedom of his clients.

While a member of the Pennsylvania General Assembly, he opposed secret societies and the foes of public education. Elected to the U.S. Congress, he led the antislavery forces. As

Chairman of the powerful Ways and Means Committee in the House, he opposed President Andrew Johnson and led the fight for the Fourteenth and Fifteenth Amendments. His reconstruction plan was a part of the comprehensive program for the reordering of black/white relations; however, his vision of complete reconstruction was too strong for most men. His proposal for "40 acres and a mule" is still quoted today. Thaddeus Stevens never married. Lydia Smith, a beautiful black woman widowed with two children, served as Stevens' housekeeper both in Washington and Lancaster until his death. It is said, although there is no proof, that Stevens was smitten with Mrs. Smith. As she presided over his homes, she was constantly spoken of as Mrs. Stevens and he made provisions for her to be buried next to him. In his will he directed that she could receive either five hundred dollars per year for life or five thousand dollars in one lump sum and that she was entitled to remove all the furniture that she considered hers "without further proof." Mrs. Smith was not buried with Thaddeus Stevens. Stevens insisted on being buried in a black

graveyard. His body is concealed in Shreiners Cemetery on Chestnut and Mulberry Streets in Lancaster. The marker on his tombstone reads:

>*"I repose in this quiet and secluded spot, not from any natural preference for solitude, but finding other cemeteries limited by charter rule as to race. I have chosen this that I might illustrate in my death the principles which I advocate through an equality of man before his Creator."*

NORTHERN
TIER

The natural area of northeast Pennsylvania is dominated by the Delaware River, Susquehanna River and the Pocono mountains which provide resort areas that make it possible for tourism to thrive. Coal mining, lumber, farming and industry characterize the counties in this region. Scranton and Wilkes-Barre, for a time, when coal mining waned, suffered some lasting ghost town effects. Bethlehem founded by the Moravians, spews out steel needed for industry all over the country. Outside of the major towns the black population is sparse.

Counties in this northern tier such as McKean, Potter, Tioga, Bradford and Susquehanna share a border with New York state and are the least populated by black or white. This heavily wooded area is given over more to nature than industry and urbanization.

Controversial figure David Wilmont who was a congressman in 1846 and author of the *Wilmont Proviso,* was a native of Bradford County. Located on a hilltop in Bethany his home still stands. The *Wilmont Proviso* was an amendment to a bill appropriating money for a negotiation of peace with Mexico that demanded slavery be prohibited in the new territory. The Proviso was rejected, but it remains as one of the famous legal garments of American slavery.

Travelers looking for historical data and monuments of black Americans will find little evidence in Elk County or its neighbors. However, there is a legend that the Nelson Gaider house on Montmorenci Road in Ridgeway served as a station on the Underground Railroad.

It is also said that the first man to be buried in a Ridgeway cemetery was a black by the name of Bill Green who had been killed by a falling tree. The cemetery is no longer in existence.

PLACES

BETHLEHEM   *LEHIGH*

Moravians Buy Slaves, Then Hire Them

Blacks are buried side by side with whites and Indian converts in God's Acre, the old Moravian cemetery on Market Street. The black freedmen and women who were Moravian converts took part in regular religious and secular life of the community. The very first Moravian foreign mission was established among the black slaves of St. Thomas in the Virgin Islands in 1832. The Moravians also bought black slaves out of slavery and employed them as wage-earning servants.

The Moravians, a German Protestant group known formally as the Unitas Fratrum, founded Bethlehem in 1741 as a missionary center for the conversion of North American Indians and others who had no formal church affiliation. Among the members of the first Moravian settlement at Bethlehem, was a black man, Andreas der Mohr, or Andrew the black. Andrew often participated in an activity assigned the "single men" to partake in the Saturday evening serenade by singing religious hymns outside of the religious sect building complex.

In 1747, four other blacks joined the religious sect—Maria Magdalena, Jupiter, Johannes, and another black named Andrew. Moravian College today is still known for its musical activities. Several black families living today in the Bethlehem, Easton, and Allentown area can trace their genealogy to slaves freed by the Moravians.

BIDDLE HILL   *SCHUYLKILL*

Hero Of Pottsville

Biddle Hill was named for the black Nicholas Biddle who, while marching in the Union Army through Baltimore on April 18, 1861, was struck in the face by a brickbat thrown by a town hoodlum. Tradition tells that this was the first blood shed in the Civil War. In spite of this injury, Nicholas Biddle survived the War by many years.

Inscribed on his tombstone behind the Bethel A.M.E. Church at Ninth and Laurel Streets in Pottsville are the following words:

> *In memory of Nicholas Biddle, Died August 2, 1876, age 80 years. His was the Proud Distinction of Shedding the First Blood in the Late War for the Union, Being Wounded While Marching Through Baltimore With the First Volunteers From Schuylkill County 18 April 1861. Erected by his Friends in Pottsville.*

A bronze plaque commemorating Biddle was placed in Garfield Square, in Pottsville; however, on the one hundredth anniversary of the day he shed the first blood marching to save the Union, his tombstone was broken in half by vandals.

EASTON   *NORTHAMPTON*

Lafayette College

Situated on a hill in the oldest section of Easton, Lafayette College stands as a symbol to the Marquis de Lafayette, a French nobleman who volunteered his services to Washington's forces during the Revolutionary War. General Lafayette said in a letter, "I would never have drawn my sword in the cause of America, if I could have conceived that thereby I was founding a land of slavery."

Among the blacks who served with the General, there was a Virginia slave by the name of James Armistead. As a spy, Armistead won the trust of the British General Cornwallis. After the surrender at Yorktown, when Cornwallis visited Lafayette's headquarters, he was amazed to see Armistead in service with Lafayette.

Armistead

Lafayette

From its humble beginnings in an old farm house in 1832, Lafayette set the standards for integration in Pennsylvania colleges, by permitting Aaron Hoff, a black man and Lafayette's first black student, to call the original forty-three students, from nearby fields, by blowing a few sounds on a horn. Lafayette was the first college in the United States to establish a Chair of Civil Rights, as a gift to the college from Fred Morgan Kirby in 1919.

MONTROSE   *SUSQUEHANNA*

Underground Railroad Activity

Black inhabitants played important roles in the development of Susquehanna County. They were instrumental in running blacks through the Underground Railroad and were fighters in the Revolutionary War. A sizeable group of blacks in Brooklyn Township was headed by landowner Prinz Perkins. Bristol Sampson was another large landowner who came to the area under the John Nicholson Land Grants. Old records show that Sampson was a war veteran and an attendant to General George Washington.

Also of that area were Isaac and David Post, agents in the Underground Railroad, who provided land for those fugitives who wanted to settle in that county. In the Civil War, twenty-five black men from Montrose joined the Union Army. The Montrose Cemetery is the site of many black burials, among which is a tombstone of a former slave that reads: "Born in Slavery—Died in Freedom."

Montrose is remembered as the home of Dr. Belle Price, an authority on wildlife, particularly wild birds. She perfected a method of combating diseases in wild birds and animals.

SMETHPORT   *McKEAN*

Tar And Feathers For Slave Owners

As early as 1827, Smethport was an important way station on the Underground Railroad. Escaped slaves *en route* north and to Canada, having struck the Allegheny River at Warren, could take a short cut through Smethport, Eldred, and Olean and were helped on to Buffalo. In the cellar of the old Medbury house in Smethport the remains of a hiding hole can still be seen.

One dramatic and ironic escape incident was recorded in the county history published in 1890. Four weary and footsore fugitive slaves stopped at David Young's hotel in Smethport where they were given a good meal as well as money quickly raised in town to help them on their way. They were directed on to Backus at Olean and had been gone only a short time when two of their owners arrived on horseback. A messenger was sent to warn the fugitives and to lead them away from their planned refuge. When the owners reached Olean they were cheerfully directed to a wood camp where a group of waiting men treated them to a generous dose of tar and feathers. The unhappy travelers had to turn in at a hotel and recuperate for a week before they were in a condition to start their return trip to their homes.

STROUDSBURG *MONROE*

Major Underground Railroad Station

In Monroe County, where Quaker influence was strong, Stroudsburg was one of the chief stations on the freedom route to Canada. Dr. Sydendam Walter was a well-known station master on this Underground Railroad station and at the same time he was a strong supporter of the Republican Party.

The black male citizenry of Monroe County participated actively in the Civil War, serving as both volunteers and draftees in the Twenty-second, Twenty-fourth and Twenty-fifth U.S. Colored Regiments, and in Company Nine in the Eighth Colored Regiment. Military records report this regiment to have suffered heavy losses—51 killed and 252 wounded—in the battle of Oluster Swamp, Florida, on February 20, 1864.

WILKES-BARRE   *LUZERNE*

First Black Admitted To The Bar

One of the most significant events that occurred in this area during the Revolutionary War was the Wyoming Massacre which led to the Sullivan Expedition. The expedition was named after General John Sullivan who was sent by General George Washington to destroy a small group of Indians who supplied the British with men and munitions. One of the participants in the Battle of Wyoming which preceded the massacre was Gershom Prince, a black soldier, who was killed. There is a monument in the Wyoming Borough commemorating the Battle of Wyoming. It also marks the spot where Gershom Prince and other patriots were buried.

Although there was not an active Underground Railroad in the area, William Gildersleeve, a local preacher, sheltered many blacks on their way to freedom.

There are two black churches in Luzerne County, both of them located in Wilkes-Barre: Mount Zion Baptist, 105 Hill Street, and Bethel A.M.E. Church, 510 South Franklin Street.

Jonathan Jasper Wright, a native of Wilkes-Barre, represented Luzerne County as a delegate at the State Equal Rights Convention for Colored People of Pennsylvania, held in Harrisburg in 1865. Wright was the first black admitted to the Bar in Pennsylvania. After serving with the Freedman's Bureau during Reconstruction he became a community leader.

WILLIAMSPORT   *LYCOMING*

Muncie Indian Station Master

In 1772 two slaves were freed and special provisions were made by their masters for future support should the freed slaves be unable to care for themselves.

Aid to fugitive slaves was extensive and organized. The citizens of Lycoming county were generally kind to escaping slaves, hid them from pursuers, and helped them along in their flight.

Williamsport was an important station on the Underground Railroad with an active and resourceful station master. The station master, Daniel Hughes, was a Muncie Indian who married a black woman and raised a large family. He operated a canal barge and on it would transport the runaway slaves from Havre de Grâce, Maryland to Williamsport where he would hide them in a local hotel or in his home which became known as Nigger Hollow. In 1936, at the insistence of Williamsport black citizens, the City Council changed that name to Freedom Road.

Some of the fleeing blacks who had intended to go north to Canada remained and settled in the county and in Williamsport, and became respected members in the community.

In 1873, in the prosperous Williamsburg lumbering industry, a conflict arose between the industry's owners and workers and an all-black militia was called upon to prevent bloody confrontations. A tall black man, first sergeant James Washington, headed that Taylor Guard militia unit. The workers lost the Sawdust War as the confrontation was later named, but the black guards averted serious violence.

PEOPLE

Henry Harris
LYCOMING

Henry Harris, known as Black Henry, was an ex-slave who was born in 1800 and died in 1887. He had been owned by the aristocratic Baynard family of Maryland and Delaware and served as a butler at *Bohemia Manor* on the eastern shore. He bought his freedom and moved to Muncy long before the Civil War. He later bought the freedom of his wife. Together, they became famous caterers in Muncy using *Bohemia Manor's* recipes.

Six feet, six inches tall, he also served as a body servant to Captain John Bowman and successfully nursed many of the company's soldiers through typhoid fever.

Harris was a highly respected citizen throughout the county. His original walnut butler's tray was copied by many imitators.

Another black inhabitant of Muncy, John Warner, operated a Railroad station there. His distinguished group of friends included the well-known black antislavery poet and lecturer, Frances Ellen Watkins Harper. She is on record as having written the first novel in America by a black woman, *Iola LeRoy, or Shadows Uplifted,* in 1892. She once approached President Lincoln and gave him a photograph with the words, "I will give you my portrait with a white back, I should like to have yours with a greenback".

Harry and Edgar Patience   *LUZERNE*

Coal sculpture has been practiced and perfected in the Patience family for more than eighty years. Harry Patience, the son of a former slave, originally started the coal sculpture business in Pittston; it was transferred to Wilkes-Barre by Harry's fourth son Edgar. The hardness of anthracite and the craftsmanship employed in its carving have won an international reputation for a range of Edgar Patience's products.

His jewelry is worn by such heads of state as the Prime Minister of Barbados, Queen Juliana of The Netherlands, wives of U.S. presidents and legislators, and Hollywood celebrities. The chapel of Kings College in Wilkes-Barre has a 4,000 pound coal altar, and there is a coal replica of the Hoover vacuum cleaner in Canton, Ohio both sculpted by Edgar Patience.

WESTERN REGION

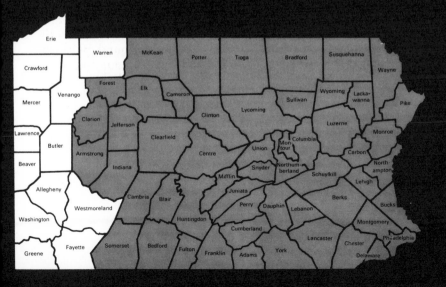

Parts of the extreme western region of Pennsylvania share borders with Lake Erie, Ohio and West Virginia. Petroleum production and natural gas is important in these counties. Titusville is the site of the first oil well in the state.

Pittsburgh, at the confluence of the Allegheny and Monongahela Rivers, is south of oil country and the center of one of the world's largest steel producing areas.

One of Pennsylvania's two National Parks, Allegheny, is an attraction for natives and tourists. It is in the vicinity of Warren, Bradford and Kane counties and is also a center for forestry research.

The nation's first for-peaceful-purposes atomic power plant is located in Shippingport (Beaver County).

Beyond the few urban areas such as Erie, very few blacks settled in the northwest part of the state. In 1922 a black doctoral student at the University of Pennsylvania noted that there were, in Franklin (Venango County), fewer than three hundred blacks among a population of seven thousand and in nearby Oil City fewer than two hundred blacks in thirteen thousand. In the surrounding countryside the proportion was even smaller.

It is a different story for the blacks in the hills and valleys of the southwest, many of whom are descended from fugitive slaves who decided to stop there in the security of wild terrain rather than go on to Canada and risk being caught on the way north. The mills of Pittsburgh and Homestead and the mines of Uniontown, Monongahela and Monessen drew black migrants.

Many blacks came to Uniontown from western Virginia during the last years of slavery, as the courthouse records fully attest. It was a popular stop on the Underground Railroad, especially Baxter Ridge, a legendary haven for fugitives. Other spots of safety were Turkey's Nest and Baker's Alley, where runaways knew that they would be protected by their fellow blacks. They also ventured out to adjoining towns, Connellsville and Greensburg, and some to Pittsburgh and beyond. Such abolitionists as John Brown, Harriet Tubman, and Frederick Douglass knew the Uniontown neighborhood very well. Among the black religious congregations were St. Paul's A.M.E. Church, on Morgantown Street.

PLACES

BROWNSVILLE   *FAYETTE*
Haven For Remaining Slaves

Located in the southwest corner of the state, Brownsville is a small industrial community situated on the slope above the Monongahela River. It was known as a boat building center during the early nineteenth century. An Anti-Slavery Society was formed here on August 19, 1826; the account of the meeting was recorded in the Washington County *Examiner.*

Bowman's Castle, an impressive former mansion, is located on the same site as Old Fort Burd. The house and grounds occupy an entire block at Second Avenue and Front Street. The original stone house was built in 1786 by Jacob Bowman as a residence and trading post. In 1847, it was renovated and enlarged. A tower was added to the huge structure which gave rise to the name of *Bowman's Castle.* The members of the Bowman family were known abolitionists. Their home served as a haven for slaves who remained in Brownsville and their descendants can be found living in the area today.

ERIE (STANTON HOUSE)   *ERIE*
Sailing Point For Ex-Slaves To Canada

Located at the southwest corner of Second and French Streets in Erie, the Stanton House was a station on the Underground Railroad. The foundation walls of the building were built with double thickness and hidden passages to secret tunnels and the water's edge, where restless slaves were quickly placed in boats and transported to Canada. For many of them Erie was their last view of the United States.

LAKE ERIE   *ERIE*
Black Seamen Vital To War Of 1812

One of the major battles of the War of 1812 against England was fought at Lake Erie. Black seamen under Commodore Oliver Howard Perry played vital and heroic roles in the bloody victory. Initially Commodore Perry objected to the use of many black sailors. He questioned their qualifications as seamen and as fighting men. However, he later paid high tribute to their bravery and courage. When this famous battle was over, he sent to General William Harrison his new thoughts about the competence of black seamen. Black musicians in the United States Navy were: George Brown, a bugler on the vessel *Chesapeake;* Cyrus Tiffany, a fifer on the *Alliance;* and Jessie Wall, a fifer on the frigate *Niagara.* Today one can see the flagship *Niagara* at a pier in Erie, Pennsylvania.

MEADVILLE   *CRAWFORD*

Main Route To Canada

Meadville was one of the main stops on the Underground Railroad system that extended from the state of Maryland through Brookville and Shippenville to Franklin, through Meadville to Lake Erie and then into Canada. John Brown, the famous abolitionist, operated a farm and tannery in nearby New Richmond, Crawford County. Brown's home was a station on the Underground Railroad.

The internationally known black scholar, W. E. B. DuBois brought prominence to Meadville when he appeared there on February 12-13, 1925. The occasion was Lincoln's birthday at which time he spoke on the black man in the history of the United States.

NEW CASTLE   *LAWRENCE*

Underground Railroad Station

Built in 1840 by the well-known abolitionist White family, the two-story brick homestead was one of the most important stops on the Underground Railroad in New Castle. Still standing at the foot of Jefferson Street Hill, the old home is now owned by St. Paul's Lutheran Church. It is said a giant Dutch oven and fireplace were constructed to feed and warm the runaways who stayed there before they were taken on to the next station.

PITTSBURGH   *ALLEGHENY*

Abolitionist Leaves Large Legacy

Avery Memorial, AME Zion Church at Nash and Avery Streets, was one of the main stations on the Underground Railroad. It derived the name from Charles Avery, abolitionist, preacher and philanthropist whose wealth came from the production of pharmaceuticals and a cotton mill. A member of the Pennsylvania Abolition Society, Avery gave large sums of money to blacks who he proclaimed were intellectually equal to whites. In 1849 he founded a college for blacks and it was known as the Allegheny Institute and Mission Church. Today, only a marker on East Ohio Street testifies to its existence. Avery died on January 17, 1858 and was buried in the *God's Acre* section of Pittsburgh's Allegheny Cemetery. There is a marble statue of Avery on his grave; on one side there is a figure of charity and the other side a figure of justice.

Avery's will provided money for Oberlin College, one of the first colleges to admit blacks. Today there is provided an Avery scholarship fund for blacks at the University of Pittsburgh.

SOUTHERN MERCER COUNTY   *MERCER*

Land Acquired For Use By Ex-Slaves

Dr. Charles Everett, an early settler and landholder of Charlottesville, Virginia, provided in his will that his thirty-nine slaves should be freed five years after his death and returned to Africa. Evidently he had a change of heart for in 1854 he acquired land for his slaves to use. The land was located in southern Mercer County near East Lackawannock, Springfield and Wilmington townships. This settlement took its name from a nearby creek and was known as Indian Run Settlement. Everett provided the necessary provisions for the blacks to erect a school and a church called White Chapel. Time has erased all indications of this settlement.

On U.S. Route 62, southwest of Sandy Lake in Mercer County there remains a marker inscribed "Freedom Road." The inscription reads:

> *"In search of freedom, men and women brought from the South by the 'Underground Railroad' settled near here about 1825 and later. After 1850 most of them went on to Canada. Their cemetery still in use, lies a short distance above the road."*

Families Aid The Underground Railroad

The village of Sugar Grove was a station on the Underground Railroad with several families involved in its operation. The William Storum family, originally from Hartford, Connecticut, migrated to Pennsylvania in 1816 and frequently played host to leading Sugar Grove citizens who were interested in the antislavery movement. It was said that the family was part Afro-American but the records are not clear.

The Underground Railroad routes in Warren County led into Chautauqua County, then into New York State. Located outside of Garland, in Spring Creek Township, Warren County, there is a natural slope called African Hill. At one time a small mill and several homes were built on the hill. Today an abandoned cemetery with over a dozen fieldstone markers is all that can be seen.

Wertz Admits Being Pilot

Three miles to the north of Waynesboro in what is now Quincy, Pennsylvania, there was a station of the Underground Railroad operated by the Wertz family. Hiram Wertz delivered a descriptive paper on the Railroad operation to the Kittochtinny Historical Society on March 29, 1911. He estimated that "from the time I first assumed the Captaincy of the Underground Railroad, in 1845, I piloted at least forty-five to fifty Negroes, none of whom, to my knowledge, were captured and returned to slavery."

A small number of blacks moved to the county during and after the Civil War. The settlements remained small and some disappeared; however, black churches remain in Chambersburg, Greencastle, and Waynesboro.

Formation Of Early Antislavery Society

West Middletown had one of the first antislavery societies in that corner of the Commonwealth since December 1823, when a notice appeared in the local county newspaper calling for the formation of a society at a meeting of interested citizens at the courthouse on January 26, 1824.

West Middletown was a major spot on the Underground Railroad where a number of routes came together. Nearby Penitentiary Woods and the home of the McKeever family provided safe hiding places.

PEOPLE

Selma Burke   *ALLEGHENY*

Among the artists who reached a peak during the W.P.A. period of the Franklin D. Roosevelt administration, one will find the name Selma Burke. A major sculptor in the succession of women and men who expressed themselves in wood, marble, granite and other media, Selma Burke has been widely exhibited in America and Europe.

Dr. Selma Burke, born in Mooreville, North Carolina, was an art major at Sarah Lawrence College and Columbia University. Her studies took her to Paris and Vienna.

Her best known piece is a bust and profile of Franklin Delano Roosevelt, which was commissioned by Eleanor Roosevelt in 1943 to use on the new dime. In performing this project, Dr. Burke ran into some difficulty; no profile photos of Roosevelt existed. When she requested the Recorder of Deeds for a personal sitting with the President, she was flatly refused. In spite of this delay, she wrote the following letter:

> *"Dear Mr. President:*
>
> *During the lifetime of President George Washington, the French sculptor, Houdon, was invited to come to this country. He travelled two months by boat.*
>
> *As you perhaps saw in the newspapers, I won the competition to do your bust. I live one hour by plane, two by railroad, and four by car. May I have a sitting with you?"*

Only days later, the reply came in a letter bearing the gold seal of the White House. It said:

> *"Dear Miss Burke:*
>
> *I will see you on the morning of February 22 at 10:00 a.m.*
>
> *(signed)*
> *Franklin D. Roosevelt"*

The original portrait is now in the Recorder of Deeds Building in Washington, D.C. She also once sculpted a bust of Mary McLeod Bethune, the great lady of education and civil rights.

In recent years, Dr. Burke has been a resident of Pittsburgh, where she is presently serving as a member of the Pennsylvania Council on the Arts and as co-founder of the Selma Burke Art Center in Pittsburgh. Her studio and property are located on route 202 in New Hope, Pennsylvania.

Harry T. Burleigh   *ERIE*

Nobody Knows The Trouble I've Seen has visited the lips of millions of black and white Americans. Harry Burleigh, the composer, was famous for that song and many others such as: *Deep River, Were You There?* and *Balm in Gilead.* He was born in 1866 in Erie and at a young age revealed a musical talent. His father died when he was young, and like many other blacks, had no resources for formal training, so even as a boy, Harry worked in Erie hotels when not attending school. His musical training was with black choral groups and choirs, but Harry's devotion and talent were to secure for him an honorable place among great black musicians. He earned a

scholarship to the National Conservatory of Music from which he graduated, and he soon established himself as soloist in a white Episcopal church and on the concert stage where he appeared before presidents and royalty. He composed more than 250 songs, many in the tradition of spirituals. His ballads and songs were performed by many well-known singers of his day. Among the many awards and honors Burleigh received was the Springarn Achievement Medal of the National Association for the Advancement of Colored People.

Burleigh was a charter member and the first of his ethnic group to serve on the board of directors of the American Society of Composers, Authors and Publishers.

Martin R. Delaney   *ALLEGHENY*

The dynamic father of black nationalism was born of free parents in Charlestown, West Virginia in 1812, grew up in Chambersburg, and settled in Pittsburgh with his family in 1831. He did his undergraduate work in Pittsburgh and then applied to Harvard Medical School, where he was accepted. After a year Delaney and two other blacks were dismissed from the school because of a petition signed by bigoted fellow students. Returning to Pittsburgh where he had earlier edited a black newspaper, *The Mystery,* he completed his medical studies and began his practice. Early in his professional life he defended his views on black colonization to Africa, and he later served as editor of Frederick Douglas' famous newspaper *North Star* from 1847 to 1849.

Delaney presided over the National Emigration of Colored Men, an organization which prescribed that blacks were to explore the possibility of emigrating to other continents (such as Canada, Central America, and South America). Delaney explored the Niger basin in Africa, one of his many expeditions there and published his famous *Official Report of the Niger Valley Exploring Party in 1861* upon his return. This report gave an account of the topography, climate, diseases, commerce, religions, and slave trade in a vivid commentary.

Once Delaney delivered a speech on the topic "The Fugitive Slave Act", before a group of prominent white citizens in Allegheny City, Pennsylvania. In it he stated:

> *"Honorable mayor, whatever ideas of liberty that I may have, have been received from reading the lives of your Revolutionary fathers. I have therein learned that a man has a right to defend his castle with his life, even unto that taking of life. Sir, my house is my castle; in that castle are none but my wife and my*

children, as free as the angels of heaven, and whose liberty is as sacred as the pillars of God. If any man approaches that house in search of a slave—I care not who he may be, whether constable or sheriff, magistrate or even judge of the Supreme Court—nay, let it be he who sanctioned this act to become law, surrounded by his body-guard, with the Declaration of Independence waving above his head as his banner, and the Constitution of this country upon his breast as a shield—if he crosses the threshold of my door, and I do not lay a lifeless corpse at my feet, I hope that the grave may refuse my body a resting place, and righteous Heaven my spirit a home. No! he cannot enter that house we both love."

A man of many facets, Delaney published two major books, *The Condition, Elevation, Emigration and Destiny of the Colored People of the United States, Politically Considered* (1852) and *Principia of Ethnology: The Origins of Race and Color* (1879).

During the Civil War he was the first black to be appointed to the rank of major in the United States Army.

Martin Delaney proposed to President Abraham Lincoln that there should be an army of Negroes, commanded by Negroes. He was not successful in winning President Lincoln to this proposal. After the war he worked with the Freedmen's Bureau and as a customs inspector in Charleston, South Carolina.

He died in 1885.

Hannibal Guards   *ALLEGHENY*

At the outbreak of the Civil War, the following letter was sent to General James S. Negley by a group of black Pittsburgh citizens known as the Hannibal Guards:

> "As we sympathize with our white fellow citizens at the present crisis, and to show that we can and do feel interested in the present state of affairs; and as we consider ourselves American citizens and interested in the Commonwealth of all our white fellow citizens, although deprived of all political rights, we yet wish the government of the United States to be maintained against the tyranny of slavery, and we are willing to assist in any honorable way or manner to sustain the present administration. We therefore tender to the state the services of the Hannibal Guards.
>
> Yours
>
> Capt., Samuel Sanders."

The offer of help was accepted and these and other black troops distinguished themselves in the war.

Jane Swisshelm   *ALLEGHENY*

Pittsburgh was a town of less than 5,000 inhabitants when abolitionist Jane Swisshelm was born in 1815. Her sharp, witty writing style carried her to Washington as correspondent for Horace Greeley's *Tribune*. A white antislavery newspaper publisher, Mrs. Swisshelm is best known for her colorful autobiography, *Half a Century,* published in 1880. It was a popular and significant document. The frequently erected barriers of "no women need apply" did not stop her forays into journalism and criticism. With tongue and pen she lashed out at targets of public officials and politicians. Mrs. Swisshelm was an early advocate of women's rights and temperance. She died in 1884 at the homestead on Braddock Avenue in Pittsburgh.

Henry Ossawa Tanner   *ALLEGHENY*

Henry Tanner was the first black artist to win coveted prizes at the Paris Salon. His fame was to grow after his death in 1937, and his works brought him recognition as one of the major American painters.

In honor of the abolitionist John Brown, Henry's father gave him the middle name Ossawa—which was derived from Ossawatomie, Kansas where, in 1856, John Brown sought to fight proslavery men. His father, an unusual man and bishop of the AME Church, worked his way through Avery College and provided the inspiration and background for Henry's fascination for religious paintings. Bishop Tanner moved his family to Philadelphia when young Tanner was an adolescent and it was in Fairmount Park that young Tanner saw artists working and decided that he too must paint.

For a short time he studied with Thomas Eakins at the Pennsylvania Academy of Fine Arts. He arranged to go to France where he lived a hand-to-mouth existence, selling only a few paintings. Convinced that he must achieve success in the art capital of the world at that time, he slowly won honors and recognition both there and in America. However, it was the painting of such religious subjects as *Daniel in the Lion's Den, Christ and Nicodemus, The Raising of Lazarus,* and *The Annunciation* that won him distinction in Europe.

Some of Tanner's other works reveal his deep interest in his own black heritage. Two examples are *The Banjo Lesson* and *The Young Sabot Maker* (wooden shoe). A few days before an exhibit of his works was scheduled to be held at the Philadelphia Museum of Art in 1970, one of Tanner's paintings, for many years thought to have been lost, turned up in the basement of the Pennsylvania School for the Deaf in Philadelphia. The work, entitled *The Thankful Poor*, depicts a black man and his son seated at a table.

Robert L. Vann ALLEGHENY

A Pittsburgh pickle factory worker started a two page sheet to air his occasional poetry. The popularity of this insignificant newspaper caught the imagination of struggling young Robert Vann, a recent graduate of the University of Pittsburgh Law School. He raised enough capital to print the first edition of the *Pittsburgh Courier*, March 10, 1910. Over the years the *Courier* grew and hundreds of people found employment in its various branch offices. Most importantly, many of today's well-known black authors were able to learn the journalism trade when the doors of white newspapers and magazines denied blacks employment. The journalism scene has shown little progress since that time.

While the paper grew Robert Vann's legal career blossomed. North Carolina born Vann was city solicitor in Pittsburgh. As early as 1924 he was an alternate delegate-at-large to the National Republican Convention. Upon switching from the Republican to the Democratic Party at the end of the Depression, he was appointed assistant U.S. attorney general by Franklin D. Roosevelt. The battleship *S.S. Robert L. Vann* was named in his honor during World War II. He died in 1940.

PHILADELPHIA COUNTY

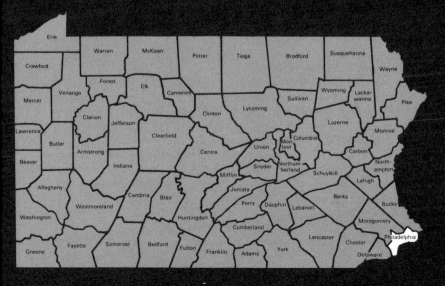

Nestled between the Schuylkill and Delaware Rivers, Philadelphia County began as an early center of commerce. While many used Philadelphia as a gateway to settlements throughout the state, many settled in the port area.

William Penn, founder and governor of "Pensilvania" (which meant "Penn's Woods") inaugurated unique relations with the Indians and, as peace reigned in the county, the term, "Penn's holy experiment" was given to the area. Settlers were guaranteed religious freedom and the state's heritage of religious freedom and tolerance is today reflected in the widest possible variety of religious and ethnic groups.

Philadelphia County was an important publishing and cultural center and still remains so, with its significant amount of prestigious art museums and educational institutions, which number about forty-five, second only to Boston.

Philadelphia is often referred to as the cradle of the country. Independence Square is the most historic square mile in the United States and part of a national historic park. For ten years, 1790-1800, it served as the nation's capital.

General information describes Philadelphia as a leading industrial center and tourist attraction. One of the world's most vital seaports, it shares with Chester a concentration of ship building.

It is the chief location of the state's textile production. It maintains the country's largest landscaped park and the oldest zoo, which is open year round.

Because there was emphasis on publishing and cultural endeavors in the early days, blacks had the best chance to benefit from the strong antislavery impulses of concerned white citizens. Also, the free blacks developed leaders among themselves, men and women who were never willing to turn their backs on their fellow blacks. Philadelphia still produces a large share of today's black artists and leaders.

PEOPLE

Richard Allen

Richard Allen was the founder of the AME (African Methodist Episcopal) Church. A germinal figure in the separate church movement, he was not the originator. Several African Baptist churches had sprung up in South Carolina and Georgia before Allen and Absalom Jones made history in Philadelphia. In summary, Richard Allen symbolized collective action—the point of power.

Born in 1760 of a "pure African" father and mulatto mother, his family, originally owned by the Benjamin Chew family, was sold to a man named Stokely, on a plantation in Dover, Delaware. Tradition tells that Allen helped convert his master to the "ways of God." Stokely permitted him and his brothers to hire out. Wisely he saved his money, bought his freedom and headed for Pennsylvania, New Jersey and Maryland, pausing to preach and earn his food by manual labor.

One Sunday in 1787, a group of black Christians were pulled from their knees while praying in front of a Methodist church in Philadelphia. Because of this, Richard Allen and

Absalom Jones mobilized to form the Free African Society of Philadelphia. Scholar DuBois called it, "the first wavering step of a people toward organized group life."

Out of the Society came the Free African Church of St. Thomas (Episcopal) with Absalom Jones as the Rector, and Bethel Methodist Episcopal Church with Richard Allen as the guiding light. In 1816 Bethel became an independent church. Today Bethel Church is commonly referred to as Mother Bethel. In the same year sixteen Methodist leaders from independent church groups formed a national organization of the African Methodist Episcopal Church. Although Allen was the prime mover of the AME Church, he was not chosen as its first bishop. According to tradition, the elected bishop, light-skinned Daniel Coker, was too fair for some of the delegates and was persuaded to step down. Allen took his place.

Allen lived his life attacking the country's conscience, working along side of his friends Absalom Jones and James Forten and raising six children with his wife, Sarah. Allen was able, despite his age, to chair the first black convention in American history (Convention of the People of Colour of the United States), which opened with forty delegates at Bethel Church. He died March 26, 1831 before the second convention.

In 1787 both Richard Allen and Absalom Jones participated in the organization of a black Masonry lodge in Philadelphia. Prince Hall, a prominent black from Boston, who founded the world's first lodge of black Masonry, presented a charter for the Philadelphia lodge at Allen's Church.

Marian Anderson

Contralto singer Marian Anderson, through her music, has brought beauty to many lives and opened doors for other black artists to achieve prominence and success. She was born in Philadelphia in 1902, one of three daughters of poor parents.

Her formal vocal training began about the age of fifteen years. Along with three hundred other young people, she entered a competition and won first prize. This led to a concert tour and an appearance with the New York Philharmonic Orchestra. Her continental debut was made in Germany in 1929.

Easter Sunday, 1939, her planned appearance at a concert in Constitution Hall in Washington, D.C. was barred by the DAR (Daughters of the American Revolution). Despite this racial insult, 75,000 people of all races, creeds and colors gathered at the Lincoln Memorial to hear her perform. Mrs. Eleanor Roosevelt, wife of President Franklin Roosevelt, resigned from the DAR because of the scandal.

Marian Anderson was the first black to perform at the Metropolitan Opera. A symbol of black pride, Marian Anderson won adulation from presidents, emperors and heads of state. A recreation center in South Philadelphia today bears her name.

Robert Bogle

The American style of "good eating" was exemplified at the tables of Robert Bogle's establishment. In 1813, near the northwest corner of Eighth and Sansom Streets, one could find Bogle's restaurant. Stately and polished in manner, he was the leading caterer of his day. Bogle was especially skilled in making meat pies but it was as a master of ceremonies at weddings and funerals that he was best known. His clients were usually quite wealthy. He always took charge of Nicholas Biddle's elaborate entertainments. Biddle, who was a banker and a poet, wrote a verse in honor of Bogle, called *An Ode to Bogle* in 1829:

> *Bogle not he whose shadow flies*
> *Before a frighted Scotsman's eyes*
> *But, thou of Eighth and Sansom, Thous*
> *Colorless, colored man whose brow*
> *Unvomed the hoy of life surveys,*
> *Untouched the gloom of death displays*
> *Reckless if joy or grief prevail!*
> *Stern multifarious Bogle, bail!*

Bogle died in 1848, on Pine Street above Tenth, leaving a daughter, Amelia.

Bustill Family

There is located in the northwest section of Philadelphia, an area whose name goes back more than two hundred years into American history. Bustleton takes its name from the Bustill family whose ancestry was a mixture of black, Indian and English. The Bustill family founded Burlington, New Jersey in 1677. Cyrus Bustill, born a slave in Burlington in 1732 bought his freedom and perfected the art of baking. Later he moved to Philadelphia and established a business at 56 Arch Street. His daughter Grace lived next door and operated a millinery store with the help of her half-Indian mother, Elizabeth.

During the Revolutionary War, Cyrus Bustill transported bread to General George Washington's half-starved army at Valley Forge. It is said that Bustill received a silver piece as a souvenir from Washington.

Bustill with Richard Allen, Absalom Jones and James Forten, was a founder of the Free African Society in 1787, the first brotherhood and mutual aid society organized by blacks in America. Although he was a Quaker, Bustill donated funds to the Society's treasury to be used for the building of the St. Thomas African Episcopal Church.

He retired from business, built a home where he opened a school, and taught black youths.

The site of his former residence was located on Third and Green Streets. The Bustills raised a family of eight children. Several became teachers and seamen. Cyrus' grandson, Joseph C. Bustill, while teaching school in Harrisburg, served as a conductor on the Underground Railroad. One Bustill became a painter and it is said that President Abraham Lincoln posed for him. Still another, Robert, studied in London at the National Gallery of Fine Arts.

Maria Luisa Bustill great-great-granddaughter of Cyrus, was the mother of Paul Robeson.

Cyrus Bustill is buried in a family plot, the site that once was his former *Edge Hill Farm* in Bustleton. The Bustill family's genealogy is a monument to black family stability.

Octavius V. Catto

In Octavius V. Catto, Philadelphia blacks had a brilliant political leader, whose early death in 1871 they mourned agonizingly just as, almost a hundred years later, blacks mourned the slaughter of Dr. Martin Luther King.

Catto was born in a well educated black Philadelphia family. He was a member of the first graduating class, and later taught, at the Institute for Colored Youth. He was actively

involved and very influential in a political organization of black voters. Catto was well respected by both whites and blacks in the city. During election time in October 1871, while working to rally black support for the Republican party, he was murdered in a street riot. Catto held a Commission as a major in the infantry of the Union Army (in an all black outfit). He was buried with full military honors. His death had a tremendous and unforseen impact, men wept like children, and the entire black community mourned for him. The U.S. Marines had to be called in to prevent race riots and Catto's body, which lay in state at the Armory at Broad and Race Streets, was guarded by the militia. The funeral was the largest in the city since President Lincoln's.

James Derham

Born a slave in Philadelphia in 1762, James Derham was the country's first black physician. As a child he was sold away from his family to Dr. John Kearsley, Jr., who sought a young slave to be trained as his assistant. At the time of the Revolutionary War, Dr. Kearsley enlisted on the side of the British army and "donated" the services of his slave, Derham to the medical unit of the 16th British Regiment. In 1781 James Derham was sold again to Dr. Robert Dove of New Orleans. Derham's medical experience continued to grow until 1783 when Dr. Dove, impressed by James' medical skills, gave him the title "doctor" and his freedom.

With a knowledge of French and Spanish, Dr. Derham was able to develop a large and successful practice and a specialty in tropical diseases which at that time were very prevalent in New Orleans. Derham lived until 1820.

James Forten

During his lifetime James Forten was one of Philadelphia's most influential black residents. He was born in 1766 and lived at 92 Lombard Street. During the American Revolution he served as a powder boy under Stephen Decatur, Commander of the Pennsylvania *Royal Louis*. After leaving the Navy, Forten established a very successful business manufacturing sails. It is estimated that his wealth exceeded $100.000, an enormous sum for any man at that time. He employed forty black and white craftsmen in his business at 95 Wharf Street.

Forten was active politically and in antislavery causes. During the War of 1812 when the British forces threatened Philadelphia, Forten, Richard Allen and Absalom Jones organized two thousand black men to erect defenses at Gray's Ferry on the Schuylkill River. The recruits assembled at the State House Yard, within hours of being called to duty to help save Philadelphia. Forten's recruiting efforts were used to solicit many of the 1700 black subscribers of William Lloyd Garrison's newspaper, *The Liberator*.

Forten frequently spoke from the pulpit of Bethel Church. He was one of the major movers who set up the first Negro Convention in Philadelphia in 1830. The Humane Society presented Forten with a certificate of appreciation for his rescue of four persons from drowning in the Delaware River on four different occasions. James Forten died in 1842.

The Forten home was a mecca for abolitionists. The Forten legacy of philanthropic concern for black people was continued by his children and grandchildren. Grandchild Charlotte Forten, educated at home and in Salem, Massachusetts, volunteered to go to Sea Island, Georgia to teach black children. She returned to Philadelphia in 1864 where she taught school and wrote for magazines. Charlotte Forten married the Reverend Francis Grimke. Her *Journal,* which she began in her school years in Salem, is an unusual record and an important historical document.

Meta Vaux Warrick Fuller

Art history shows that two women sculptors followed the distinctive style and creativity of the country's first black female sculptor, Edmonia Lewis; Meta Vaux Warrick Fuller and May Howard Jackson, both born in Philadelphia in 1877.

Although Mrs. Fuller received training in Philadelphia, she migrated abroad where she attracted the attention of the art world. Her work won applause from the great French sculptor and painter, Auguste Rodin.

The Wretched, exhibited in Paris in 1903, portrayed human torment, and is generally regarded as her masterpiece. She chose to depict the horrible, the gruesome, the tragedy of life rather than the joy. However, one of her best pieces was made for the Jamestown Tercentennial and represented the advancement of blacks since their landing at Jamestown in 1619.

Meta was proud of her black heritage. In researching her genealogy she discovered that her great-great-grandmother was an African princess, brought to Philadelphia on a slave ship, and sold to a wealthy family in the city. It is stated that her owners were so captivated by her beauty that a white husband was found for her. Meta's father was a barber and her mother worked as a hairdresser.

As wife of Dr. Solomon Fuller, she continued to produce works in keeping with the black experience.

Mifflin Gibbs

Son of a Methodist minister, Mifflin Gibbs was born in Philadelphia in 1828. As a young person he became involved in the Underground Railroad and antislavery movement and was persuaded, at age twenty, by Frederick Douglass to lecture around the country. The California Gold Rush called him, as it did many seeking a fortune. Among other things that he was to do in California, Gibbs started a clothing store business, but not before he shined shoes in front of the Union Hotel in San Francisco. Attracted to politics, Gibbs saw the

need for a black newspaper. In 1855 he published *Mirror of the Times* which continued for a number of years insuring Gibb's active role in protest movements of the day—one of which was the poll tax levy on blacks. Because he refused to pay the poll tax, his store inventory was confiscated and put up for auction. During the auction a white man addressed the audience with the explanation of the situation. Consequently, no one bid, and the stock was returned to Gibbs and his partners.

By 1866 Gibbs moved to Canada and was elected a councilman. From there he went to Oberlin College in Ohio and finally to the Arkansas Bar. He became the country's first black judge—a municipal judge in Little Rock in 1873. Near the end of his career he was appointed a U.S. Consul to Madagascar.

His autobiography is called *Shadow and Light*.

Elizabeth Taylor Greenfield

This remarkable black singer was born in Natchez, Mississippi, in 1809 and was later adopted by a Quaker woman who brought her to Philadelphia. Elizabeth's guardian encouraged and enabled her to study music. Her singing career began with performances at local parties. Her performance before the Buffalo Musical Association in 1851 brought her immediate attention; newspaper critics named her the Black Swan, and the affectionate title remained with the singer throughout her life. Her voice was often compared to that of the Swedish singer, Jenny Lind. Her range and lyrical quality resulted in the appellation African Nightingale. Elizabeth Taylor Greenfield gave concerts in all the eastern states. A tour in England in 1854 was climaxed by a performance at Buckingham Palace at the personal request of Queen Victoria.

May Howard Jackson

At a time when black artist Meta Vaux Warrick was lured to European shores, May Jackson, a black sculptor, found Philadelphia a place in which to create. Born the same year (1877) as Meta Warrick in Philadelphia, May Jackson excelled in portraits of forthright men. Her bust of Kelly Miller, a prominent black orator, is perhaps her most well-known work.

Frank Johnson

Philadelphia was the home of Frank Johnson, a well educated musician born with a talent for organization and leadership. The Duke Ellington of his day, Johnson built a reputation in the mid 1800s as a composer, band leader, fiddler, bugler and orchestra director. Johnson was a member of the first all black military band organized in Philadelphia in 1821. He had the good fortune to play for General Lafayette at the Chestnut Street Theatre in 1825; at which time Lafayette was so impressed with Johnson that he sponsored a European tour for him. While on tour he was invited to play for Queen Victoria. Highly pleased with his musicianship, she presented him with a silver bugle. When he died in 1844 the bugle was placed upon his coffin and buried with him.

Absalom Jones

Born a slave in Sussex, Delaware on November 6, 1746, Absalom learned to read as a child. At sixteen he was taken to Philadelphia to work in his master's shop where a clerk taught him how to write. In 1766 he was allowed to attend night school. His savings enabled him to first purchase his wife's freedom and then his own. The couple continued in the employ of their former master.

In the process of time Jones became a friend of Richard Allen and together they founded the Free African Society which served as a protective society and social organization for free blacks. Disputes arose concerning leadership of the religious rites for the Society and Jones was awarded the post. Jones and Allen, both inclined to preach, were part of St. George's Methodist Church. Harassed by the white Methodists, Jones and Allen made a decision to organize blacks outside of the church and so the Free African Society was established. Absalom Jones, Richard Allen and other black Methodists shared a humiliating experience at St. George's when they were literally chased from the Church.

Toward the end of 1790 Absalom Jones and Richard Allen were encouraged by Benjamin Rush to inaugurate a separate black church. An election was held in the Free African Society to decide what denomination the church would be. The large majority voted for the Church of England. Absalom accepted

the pastorate and in 1794 the African Church of St. Thomas opened. Shortly thereafter, the church started an insurance company. In 1804, it organized a day school for young people and in 1809, it set up a society for the suppression of vice. During the Yellow Fever epidemic, they jointly wrote: *A Narrative of the Proceedings of the Black People, During the Late Awful Calamity in Philadelphia, 1794* to rebutt the slanderous misrepresentation of black folks' involvement during the city-wide disaster. Dr. Rush, in charge of mobilizing fifty physicians during the epidemic, called on Absalom Jones to organize the nursing of the sick. Allen was to supervise burials. William Gray, another black leader, assisted in organizing blacks to work in the city's recovery.

In 1799 Absalom Jones and seventy-five other black men sent a petition through a representative in Congress, Robert Wain of Pennsylvania, who petitioned the United States Congress against the slave trade, the Fugitive Slave Act of 1793, and against slavery itself. Although the petition failed to protect the rights of blacks held in slavery, the petition was the first official protest to the United States Congress by blacks in America. This is recorded to have been the first public defense by free blacks in America.

In 1814 when the British were threatening Philadelphia, Absalom Jones and Richard Allen were called upon to recruit black fighters. Two thousand, five hundred black folk marched to Gray's Ferry and manned the defenses.

Jones died in 1818.

Jarena Lee

Stimulated to preach the gospel during her early years, Jarena Lee worked to earn her livelihood as a maid and an itinerant preacher. She was born in Cape May, N.J. in 1783.

Upon arriving in Philadelphia she was encouraged to exercise her talent for speaking by Bishop Richard Allen of Mother Bethel Church, who was an early advocate of women's liberation and equality. He gave her an opportunity to preach at his church.

While traveling throughout the eastern seaboard, Jarena in one year preached 178 sermons. She covered 2,325 miles under adverse conditions to deliver her words of wisdom and inspiration. For a short period she lived in Pittsburgh. The citizens of Norristown were so pleased with a sermon she preached in 1824 that she was asked to return to preach at the Academy, located on DeKalb Street opposite Airy Street.

She married Joseph Lee, pastor of a society at Snow Hill, six miles from Philadelphia.

Dorothy Ripley, another brilliant black preacher, was permitted to conduct sermons in 1803 by Bishop Allen. However, Jarena has the honor of being known as the "first female preacher" of the First African Church in the United States.

Alain Locke

Few blacks have been able to take advantage of what Cecil Rhodes took out of Africa and turned in to what the academic world gives for excellence—the Rhodes Scholarship.

Alain Locke, native of Philadelphia, was one of those few. In 1907 he went to Oxford as a Rhodes Scholar. John Wideman of Pittsburgh and Joseph Stanley Sanders of Los Angeles were also chosen for this distinction. More than several blacks have made the semi-finals. After attending the University of Berlin, he joined the faculty at Howard University in 1912.

Dr. Alain Locke's intellectual influence extended way beyond the campus of Howard University. He took up pen and typewriter to reach hungry black minds and produced works about the achievements and influence of blacks. His philosophical works include: *The Problem of Classification in the Theory of Value* and *Imperatives in American Philosophy: Today and Tomorrow.* Also published were: *The Negro in America* (1933), *The Negro and His Music* (1936), *Negro Art: Past and Present* and *The Negro in Art* (1941).

Locke was the first black to be elected president of the National Council of Adult Education. He died before he could finish *The Negro in American Culture.* Margaret Just Butcher completed the work. When black authors speak of black scholars, Alain Locke is frequently one of the first mentioned. A catalyst in shaping the Harlem Renaissance, he was qualified to be called "critic" in a time when there were few black critics. His positions on ancestral legacy and his emphasis on Africa and folk contributions anticipated the posture of militant and revolutionary thinking blacks today.

Robert Purvis

Robert Purvis was a most influential and very handsome black leader of his time. Born in 1810 in Charleston, South Carolina, he was of English, African, and Jewish extraction. His wealthy white father sent him at an early age to Philadelphia, where he had established a private school for black children. Robert attended Amherst College in New England, where he met the noted abolitionist William Lloyd Garrison. Partly influenced by Garrison's writings, Purvis devoted his life to the liberation of blacks. He also became an advocate of women's rights. When, in 1838, the Pennsylvania legislature enacted that blacks be deprived of the right to vote, Purvis made an appeal in a published document entitled, *Appeal of Forty Thousand Citizens Threatened with Disfranchisement to the People of Pennsylvania.* Through lecturing and writing, involvement in a number of antislavery societies, and service as an agent for the Underground Railroad, Purvis fought for blacks. He raised cattle on his farm in Chester County; however his residence was in a section of Philadelphia called Byberry.

Purvis' son, Charles Burleigh Purvis, was the first Philadelphia black to graduate from medical school at Western Reserve School of Medicine in Cleveland, Ohio, in 1864. Philadelphia would not admit blacks into its medical colleges at that time. Dr. Charles Purvis was appointed as acting assistant surgeon in the United States Army. After his discharge from service, he joined the staff at Howard University in Washington, D.C.

Paul Robeson

Even as a poor minister's son in Princeton, New Jersey, Paul Robeson had a profound concern for the little man. After years of exercising his many talents all over the world, he returned to the inhospitable climate of this country and took up residence in West Philadelphia where few are aware of his presence. He is perhaps better known in other lands. He visited Russia where he was honored and when he spoke of that experience he said, "For the first time I walked the earth in complete dignity there." At one time as an actor, singer and activist, Robeson was the toast of the town. It was not long after that success that his passport was taken away and the art world black-listed him into artistic silence.

A Phi Beta Kappa student at Rutgers, Paul Robeson was known for his athletic prowess. An all-American end in 1917

and 1918, he also played basketball and baseball and was a track star. The earning of a law degree at Columbia University was not the beginning of a law practice as would be expected. He caught the acting bug and his first part was that of a cross bearer in a Harlem YMCA production. During this period and without the benefit of formal singing lessons he simultaneously began a singing career which took him on tour abroad. In the early days of film, Robeson was seen in *Emperor Jones, Showboat, Jerico,* and *King Solomon's Mines.* He is remembered for the stage production of *Othello.*

In 1930 the executive committee of the Art Alliance (Philadelphia) returned Antonio Salemme's bronze, nude statue of Paul Robeson which they invited the artist to submit in competition with the works of other nationally known artists. The committee feared for the consequences of exhibiting a Negro nude statue in a public square (Rittenhouse Square). Since that incident the Art Alliance has exhibited the work of some black artists.

Having studied twenty languages, including Chinese and Russian, he has had the blessing of being able to sing and converse in native tongues around the world.

In 1938 Robeson sang before the International and Abraham Lincoln Brigades in Madrid, Spain during the Spanish Civil War. Loud speakers were erected so that opposing armies could hear him—the guns remained silent while his commanding voice was heard in song.

During World War II Robeson was a leader in the entertainment world's drive to sell war bonds.

Paul Robeson's accomplishments surely earn him the title, "Renaissance Man."

Prince Saunders

Of the various personalities who achieved prominence in Philadelphia, Prince Saunders is one of the least known by today's scholars. Although born of free black parents in Vermont, Saunders became one of the most renowned educators, lecturers, and politicians of his day. After first teaching school in a free black school in Colchester, Connecticut, and then in Boston's African Meeting House from 1809 to 1812, he went on to found Boston's prestigious African Institution.

In 1818 Saunders came to Philadelphia and became affiliated with St. Thomas's African Episcopal Church. Reverend William Douglass wrote an illuminating account of him in his *Annals of the First African Church,* Philadelphia, 1862:

>*He was said to be of pure African blood, unprepos-
>sessing in his external appearance, but of highly
>polished manners and of brilliant parts. He was born
>in this country, but his uncommon brightness, while a
>youth, drew the attention of some influential and
>wealthy friend, who as an experiment, had him sent to
>England to be educated;—and the proficiency he had
>there made, more than met the most sanguine expec-
>tations of his friends.*

While continuing his education in London a few years earlier, Saunders became acquainted with two prominent British
abolitionists, Thomas Clarkson and William Wilberforce, who
were advocates of black freedom.

Saunders later emigrated to Haiti and became a *confidant* of
the eminent black king, Henri Christophe. Saunders vacci-
nated and taught the king's children. Christophe was so impressed with Saunders that he appointed him as his Minister
of Education.

In 1816 Saunders returned to London. During the same year
he edited and published the *Haitian Papers*. These papers
were a collection of the Code Henri, consisting of a proclamation, official documents, and an account of the rise, progress,
and present state of the kingdom of Haiti.

After publication of the two hundred and twenty-eight page
volume, Saunders returned to Haiti. He was dismissed as
minister by the furious king for having published the papers
without the king's permission.

Saunder's first publication in Philadelphia was *An Address
Delivered at Bethel Augustine Society for the Education of
People of Colour,* which was delivered on September 3, 1818.
The members of the newly organized society were so im-
pressed by Saunders' eloquent address that they asked his
permission to publish it.

Later that same year Saunders published his second work in Philadelphia entitled *A Memoir Presented to the American Convention for the Promotion of Slavery.*

Upon hearing the news of the dramatic and tragic suicide of King Christophe, Saunders returned to Haiti in 1820, where he once again rose to power. At the time of his death in 1839, Saunders was the Attorney General of Haiti.

Stephen Smith

Stephen Smith was a lumber merchant, fuel supplier, and real estate dealer who was said, in his time, to have been the wealthiest black in the United States. Born in 1795 in Columbia, Pennsylvania, Smith built an empire that included Smith, Whipper & Co., which had a lumber yard at Broad Street above Willow, and a coal yard at Broad Street above Callowhill.

While William Whipper, a relative and business partner, attended to the business of the lumber and coal yard, Smith involved himself in other ventures. He invested in real estate and owned over fifty brick houses in the city of Philadelphia. He made generous contributions to charity groups.

In 1867, he donated property and cash worth $250,000. for the establishment of a Home for the Aged and Infirmed. The Home, which bears his name, still operates at Forty-fourth Street and Girard Avenue. It was dedicated in 1871, two years before Smith died.

John H. Smythe

Immediately following Reconstruction times, John H. Smythe was one of the earliest ministers to Libeiia (Africa). He represented other governments during his term there. (Belgium, Germany, Sweden and Norway). History writes that Smythe was the first black newsboy in Philadelphia and the first black artist to become a member of the Philadelphia Academy of Fine Arts. He studied at the Institute of Colored Youth, headed by Ebenezer Bassett, who was the first black minister to Haiti. After attending Howard University's Law School, he worked in a succession of jobs that included the Freedmen's Bureau and Internal Revenue. Following his tour abroad he resumed a law practice in Washington, D.C. and died in 1908.

William Still

William Still was one of the most successful black businessmen in Philadelphia's history. He was born in New Jersey in 1821, the last of eighteen children of Levin and Sidney Still and came to Philadelphia in 1844. Still taught himself to read and write, and in 1847, he took a job as a clerk in the office of the Pennsylvania Anti-Slavery Society. Later, he became an abolitionist and was a famous figure in the Underground Railroad. By 1867, he had a prosperous coal and lumber yard at 1216-1220 Washington Avenue and an office at 413 Lombard Street. Still was one of the organizers of the first YMCA for black people in America.

In 1851 William Still celebrated a joyful reunion with his brother, Peter, who had been kidnapped from the doorsteps of his home in New Jersey and was sold as a slave forty years before in the southern states of Kentucky and Alabama. Peter Still was aided by the heroic efforts of two Jewish brothers, Joseph and Isaac Friedman of Alabama who made contacts for him and his wife Vina to escape to the north on the Underground Railroad.

Peter Still was taken to the Anti-Slavery Office in Philadelphia where he related his story to William Still who was the secretary of the Anti-Slavery Society. The secretary was shocked with emotion as he heard the dramatic tale from the fugitive slave who was his lost brother. A detailed sketch of this breath-taking event is revealed in *The Kidnapped and the Ransomed*, originally published in 1856 by Kate Pickard, and reprinted by the Jewish Publication Society of America in 1970.

In 1860 William Still went into the coal stove business and earned a modest fortune. He was elected to the Board of Trade in Philadelphia. Before his death in 1902 he was the author of the much read classic, the *Underground Railroad* published in 1872. Still, an efficient Underground Railroad station master, kept a written record of fugitives whose escapes he engineered, so that relatives and friends might locate them.

Moses Williams

Among the many black persons who contributed to the development of fine arts in this country, there was Moses Williams, an expert silhouette maker and slave of Charles Willson Peale, one of the most popular and successful painters in colonial America.

Moses Williams started out in the Peale establishment as an animal feeder. Promotion came later when Peale opened his museum in 1802 at Third and Lombard Streets. With the money Williams made from his silhouette proficiency, he was able to purchase his freedom. As a free man, Williams began his family life when he married the white cook of the Peale house, Marie. This union was somewhat ironic in light of Marie's former contempt for Moses when he was a slave.

THE RADICALS

Nancy Cunard

Nancy Cunard (1896-1965), a direct descendent of Benjamin Franklin, was considered a great rebel during her life time. Although considered bohemian, she was an heiress to the Cunard shipping wealth and a poet. In the 1920s and 1930s her name was a byword in both the British and American press, mostly because of her sympathy for blacks.

In 1934 she used her private press (*Hour Glass Press*) to publish *Negro*, a landmark in Afro-American literature. The book was one of the most ambitious anthologies on blacks ever attempted. It covered every aspect of black life throughout the world. The original edition consisted of 855 pages, some 259 articles by 150 contributors. Its format was large and it weighed eight pounds. Of the one thousand copies that were published, five hundred were destroyed during the bombing in England in World War II. A copy can be found at the Library Company of Philadelphia.

Benjamin Franklin

The imposing Franklin Square named for Benjamin Franklin occupies a large tract of land between Race and Vine on Sixth Street. It is one of several sites honoring the memory of Franklin in the Philadelphia area.

On the subject of blacks, Franklin's attitude was at first ambivalent. Though he printed several antislavery works during his early printing career, he did not show any great concern about the institution itself. In 1764, in a pamphlet entitled, *What is Sauce for a Goose Is Also Sauce for a Gander*, his political opponents openly accused him of keeping black paramours. He seems to have made no attempt to deny it. Shortly before the American Revolution, under the influence of two antislavery leaders, Anthony Benezet of Philadelphia and Granville Sharp of England, Franklin's attitude toward slavery changed permanently. He was elected to the Pennsylvania Abolition Society in 1787, along with Thomas Paine, and later served as the Society's president.

Franklin was a member of the Convention which formed the Constitution of the United States in 1787. In 1789 he sent a petition to Congress which he signed as president of the Pennsylvania Abolition Society, asking them to exert the full extent of the power vested in them by the Constitution in discouraging the traffic of human species.

The Grimke Sisters

Angelina and Sarah Grimke were born into a wealthy slaveholding family in Charleston, South Carolina. They were deeply anguished by the slave society that they saw all about them and they recognized its devastating effects on both slave and master. Unable to tolerate living under those conditions any longer, they eventually moved to Philadelphia, joined the Society of Friends, and became active in the abolitionist movement. In 1836 and 1837 they published pamphlets which spoke out so forcefully against slavery that slaveholders were enraged. In South Carolina the anger was directed particularly towards Angelina who was threatened with imprisonment should she return to her native state.

While living in Philadelphia, the Grimke sisters learned of the existence of two black nephews, sons of their brother and a slave woman on his estate. The sisters welcomed Francis and Archibald as relatives and helped them through Lincoln University. Francis later became a minister, a leader in the NAACP, a trustee of Howard University in Washington, D.C., and a member of the American Negro Academy. He married Charlotte Forten, the granddaughter of James Forten, a free black resident of Philadelphia who was an active abolitionist. Archibald Grimke became an author and an attorney. His daughter, named for one of his white aunts, Angelina Weld Grimke, was a well-received poet and playwright.

Thomas Paine

Thomas Paine, born in England in 1737, was the son of a Quaker farmer and a corset maker.

Paine is known primarily for his revolutionary ideas published in his own, political pamphlet-journal, *Common Sense*.

Paine was a genuine lover of liberty and bluntly attacked all forms of its abuse. He joined the Pennsylvania Abolition Society and throughout his career he spoke out emphatically against slavery. His first published article in America, in the *Pennsylvania Journal and Weekly Advertiser*, March 8, 1775, was a scathing attack on fellow Christians for practicing or condoning slavery.

William Penn

One of the largest municipal buildings in the nation occupies four and a half acres at Broad and Market and is called City

Hall. A massive seven-story building in the French Second Empire style, it is the most impressive landmark in Philadelphia with its twenty-six ton statue of William Penn, the founder of the state, rising more than 500 feet above the street on City Hall Tower. While a Quaker, Penn planned and founded a colony where all races of mankind were to enjoy religious and political freedom. William Penn had black slaves, as did some of the Penns after him. In 1701, Penn, on his return to England, liberated his slaves, stating, "I give to . . . my blacks their freedom as is under my hand already." This will, which was left with James Logan, Penn's secretary, was not carried out. Penn's last will contains no mention of his blacks. Logan and the other administrators stated that they could not follow Penn's instructions because they were a "private matter."

George Washington

Throughout his life George Washington was the master of about 300 slaves. When slaves became too difficult to control he sold them and they were marched two by two through the city as sale time approached. But Washington did have his favorite ones and history cites certain slaves such as William Lee, bought from Mary Lee in 1768. William Lee accompanied Washington through thick and thin until the Revolutionary War ended and then to the Mount Vernon household with his wife Margaret Thomas, a free woman from Philadelphia. When he died in 1799, his will provided that upon Martha Washington's death all of his slaves should be liberated, but "to my Mulatto man William (calling himself William Lee) I give immediate freedom."

During the War, Hamet Achmet was his master drum maker. Tradition tells of an occasion when Washington slept under the same blanket with Primus Hall, a black soldier serving under Colonel Pinkering. The famous picture of Washington crossing the Delaware contains a black named Prince Whipple.

In George Washington's life, next to his faithful slave William Lee, there was Francis who was born in the French West Indies of black and white parents. He was affectionately known as Black Sam. He later changed his name to Fraunces upon emigrating to New York City, and in keeping with the fashion of the times he wore a powdered wig. He owned one of the finest taverns there that became known throughout colonial America. Washington ate at his friend's tavern whenever he visited New York City. At his Richmond Hill mansion headquarters in 1776, Francis' daughter Phoebe, who was employed as the General's housekeeper, revealed a plot and saved Washington's life. She refused to serve the General a dish of his favorite green peas laced with poison. The food had been given to her by one of Washington's bodyguards, Thomas Hickey, an Irishman who was an agent for the British. Hickey was Phoebe's lover and she revealed the assassination plot after a lover's quarrel. Hickey was later hanged. When Washington arrived in Philadelphia in 1790 as President, Fraunces came with him as his personal cook and remained in Washington's service until 1794.

"Black Sam" Fraunces

Fraunces established a tavern at 166 South Second Street; however, the site was a bad choice for business. The following year he established yet another elaborate tavern at 59 South Water Street where misfortune plagued the industrious tavernkeeper once again. Heartbroken and forlorn, Fraunces died in Philadelphia in 1795, leaving a will that said that the Federal Government and several states owed him money for housing and feeding soldiers during the Revolutionary War.

The historic Fraunces Tavern in the Wall Street section of New York was the scene of a bombing January of 1975. Persons claiming membership in the Fuerzas Armadas de Liberacion Puertorriquenia called the news media to take responsibility for the bombing in which four persons were killed and at least 40 were injured.

John Greenleaf Whittier

Born in a farm house at Haverhill, Massachusetts, Whittier —the Poet Laureate of New England—displayed an early passion for the abolition of slavery along with his fellow New England writers, Harriet Beecher Stowe, Henry Wadsworth Longfellow and Ralph Waldo Emerson. Whittier, a Quaker, served as editor for two leading antislavery newspapers: William Lloyd Garrison's *The Liberator*, and *The Pennsylvania Freeman*, while living in Philadelphia. He first came to the city in December 1833, as a delegate from Massachusetts to organize the American Anti-Slavery Society. The convention of less than seventy-five people met at the Adelphi, on Fifth Street below Walnut Street. Serving as one of the convention secretaries, Whittier, along with Garrison and Samuel J. May, drafted the now famous *Declaration of Anti-Slavery Sentiments*. The document was written principally at night in the attic of a black citizen's home.

Although his Quaker coat had been pelted with eggs and his newspaper office of the *Pennsylvania Freeman* burned over his head, Whittier used to remark to visitors to his home, Oak Knoll, near Danvers, Massachusetts: "I set a higher value on my name as appended to the Anti-Slavery Declaration in 1833, than on the title page of any book."

BEGINNINGS

The Declaration of Independence

Thousands of persons pass the site at the southwest corner of Seventh and Market Streets every day; however, only a few notice a bronze tablet on the Market Street side of the present building which states that, in The Graff House, which originally stood at the corner of Seventh and Market Streets, Thomas Jefferson wrote the Declaration of Independence. The house's address was 230 High Street; later changed to 700 Market Street. In the Declaration of Independence, as it was originally written by Jefferson, both slavery and the slave trade were denounced in the most uncompromising language. Though a slave owner himself, Jefferson's clause reads as follows: (he is referring to King George III)

> *He has waged cruel war against human nature itself, violating its most sacred rights and liberty in the persons of a distant people who never offended him, captivating and carrying them into slavery in another*

> *hemisphere, or to incur miserable death in their transportation thither. This warfare, the opprobrium of INFIDEL powers is the warfare of the CHRISTIAN King of Great Britain. Determined to keep open a market where MEN should be bought and sold, he has prostituted his negative for suppressing every legislative attempt to prohibit or to restrain this execrable commerce; and that this assemblage of horrors might want no fact of distinguished die, he is now exciting these very people to rise in arms among us, and to purchase that liberty of which he deprived them, by murdering the people upon whom he also obtruded them; thus paying off former crimes committed against the liberties of one people, with crimes which he urges them to commit against the lives of another.*

The Continental Congress struck this passage from the Declaration. John Adams, who didn't like Jefferson, thought the clause was one of the best parts. Jefferson explained the reasons for the deletion by saying, "The clause reprobating the enslaving the inhabitants of Africa was struck out in complaisance to South Carolina and Georgia, who had never attempted to restrain the importation of slaves, and who, on the contrary, still wished to continue it. Our northern brethren also, I believe, felt a little tender under these censures; for though their people had very few slaves themselves, yet they had been pretty considerable carriers of them to others."

Independence Hall

Few events in our nation's history produced such a profound influence on American lives as the writing of the Constitution. The word slavery was not mentioned in the Constitution until the 13th Amendment.

The large states supported the Virginia Plan, by which a state's representation in both houses of Congress would have been determined by the population. The small states supported the New Jersey Plan, calling for equal representation in Congress. The agriculture states of the south had the greater number of slaves and they proposed that the slaves should be counted as part of the total population. However, with the question of deciding the amount of taxes, the southern planters wanted to count slaves as population. The northern states vigorously opposed this plan, finally a compromise was reached, that three out of every five slaves should be counted for purposes of representation.

> *"Representatives and direct taxes shall be apportioned among the several states which may be included within this union according to their respective numbers, which shall be determined by adding to the whole number of free persons, including those bound to service for a term of years, and excluding Indians not taxed, three fifths of all other persons."*

A second important compromise between the north and south provided that after twenty years no more slaves could be brought into this country from Africa until 1808.

> *"The migration or importation of such persons as any of the states now existing shall think proper to admit, shall not be prohibited by the Congress prior to the year one thousand eight hundred and eight, but a tax or duty may be imposed on such importation, not exceeding ten dollars per each person."*

The Liberty Bell

In Independence Hall where American liberty was claimed and proclaimed, there stands the historic symbol so reverently preserved as the noblest utterance of human rights and as the charter of freedom. First hung in 1753, the bell bore the inscription, "Proclaim Liberty throughout the Land unto all the Inhabitants thereof." How the bell got its familiar name is unknown, for throughout the years the bell was called by many names. However, the earliest reference to it as the "Liberty Bell" is connected to an extreme antislavery society in 1839, known as The Friends of Freedom, a group which called for the immediate liberation of blacks from slavery and the continued promotion of security, protection, and improvement for free blacks. Founded in Boston, the Society issued a famous series of publications, pamphlets entitled *The Liberty Bell by the Friends of Freedom.* Inscribed in the 1839 issue of the annual pamphlet is a sonnet which reads, "suggested by the inscription on the Philadelphia Liberty Bell."

> *It is no tocsin of affright we sound,*
> *Summoning nations to the conflict dire;—*
> *No fearful peal from cities wrapped in firs*
> *Echoes, at our own behest, the land around:—*
> *Yet would we rouse our country's utmost bound.*

The 1848 edition of *The Liberty Bell* is of particular interest in black history, for it contains two articles by prominent black writers. They are William Wells Brown's *The American Slave*

Trade and *Bibles for the Slaves* by Frederick Douglass. Associated with *The Liberty Bell* were Maria Weston Chapman, William Lloyd Garrison, John Greenleaf Whittier, Elizabeth Barrett Browning of England, Harriet Martineau, and other distinguished blacks and whites.

Negro Soldiers Monument

This monument, on Lansdowne Drive, West Fairmount Park, was erected in 1934 in memory of Negro soldiers of Pennsylvania who fought in the nation's wars.

The story of the black soldier is one of the neglected aspects of American history. Black and white men fought side by side in every major military engagement in our nation's history. George Washington and Andrew Jackson applauded the bravery of the black soldier, and Abraham Lincoln claimed that it was blacks who turned the balance of power for the Union's victory in the Civil War. Under Theodore Roosevelt, they fought in the battles of Santiago and San Juan Hill in the Spanish-American War, and they marched "from Pennsylvania to the Rhine River" in World War I, "the War to End All Wars".

Blacks were among the first to volunteer to defend their country in every war since the Revolutionary War. However, during the Italio-Ethiopian War, 1935-36, the United States government enforced a law that was enacted in 1818, which imposed a penalty of one thousand dollars and three years in prison on any citizen who enlisted in a foreign war. Fifteen thousand blacks from Philadelphia were among those who volunteered to defend Ethiopia.

A LEGACY OF INSTITUTIONS

Berean Institute

The Berean Institute was founded in 1899 by Dr. Matthew Anderson, a black leader who also was founder of the Berean Presbyterian Church and the Berean Savings Fund Society in Philadelphia. At the time the school was chartered by the state (1904) it was very difficult for blacks to be admitted to manual training schools. Although the school was founded primarily to serve the black community, it soon became integrated and today provides education for blacks and whites in almost equal numbers. Berean attracts a heavy number of Spanish-speaking individuals and people from foreign countries.

Berean Institute's new school is located at 1901 West Girard Avenue in Philadelphia, where it offers expanded course work in business administration, electronics, secretarial programs, and other trade programs.

Heritage House

Founded in 1949 by Dr. Eugene Waymon Jones, Heritage House is located at 1346 North Broad Street and offers educational and cultural activities to black children. Heritage House was the former home of Edwin Forrest, a Philadelphia actor, and is the oldest black cultural center in the United States.

Kunder House

Now being used as a commercial laboratory, the site of the first formal protest against slavery in North America in 1688 is located at 5109 Germantown Avenue.

Germantown had been settled by German refugees whose religious beliefs were similar to the Friends. Led by Francis Daniel Pastorius, these early Quakers wrote an historic document marking the beginning of Pennsylvania's strong moral stand early in the antislavery movement, which set the stage for the fiery abolitionist movement about seventy-five years later.

In 1688, this Germantown Meeting passed a surprising, eloquent and convincing protest against slavery. It was written by Pastorius and was sent to the Abington Quarterly Meeting. It was turned down; then forwarded to the Philadelphia Yearly Meeting where it was dropped as "radical and untimely."

Liberty Hall

Read before a large public gathering on April 8, 1867 at Liberty Hall, the largest public building owned by a black, was the historic petition, *Struggle for the Rights of the Colored People of Philadelphia in the City Railway Cars*. It was led by the noted black antislavery leader, William Still of Philadelphia, who had procured approximately 360 signatures of some of the most influential white citizens of that city.

The valiant effort by the black citizens was finally aided by the State Legislature in 1867 when it enacted a law prohibiting discrimination within the Commonwealth.

Pennsylvania Hall

Although blacks in the United States did not gain the right to vote until 1870, Philadelphia blacks were fighting for this right as early as 1836. That year, despite the large number of free blacks in Philadelphia and the fact that free blacks had been allowed to vote in Pennsylvania, anti-abolitionists succeeded in presenting to the Pennsylvania State Legislature over forty petitions opposing voting rights for non-whites. In 1837, the State Supreme Court, in the case of Fogg vs. the Electors of Luzerne County, decided the issue. Fogg was a free black seeking the right to vote. The Court ruled against him. One year later, a State Convention wrote "white" into the qualifications for voters, thus denying Pennsylvania blacks the ballot for the next thirty-three years. Bitterness led to mob violence on the streets of Philadelphia. At the height of this violence a black church at Seventh and Bainbridge Streets was burned. White mobs also burned the Shelter of Colored Orphans, at Thirteenth and Callowhill Streets. On May 17, 1838, the anti-slavery agitation center, Pennsylvania Hall, was burned by a group of pro-slavery Philadelphians. It had been erected by abolitionists and was burned the day after its first meeting. The city's police refused to provide adequate protection.

Stenton

Erected on a plantation that contained over five hundred acres is the home of James Logan, an early settler of historic Germantown and the appointed secretary to William Penn. Logan designed and built *Stenton*, as the home was called, between

1723 and 1730. *Stenton* was occupied, for a time, during the Revolutionary War by General George Washington in 1777 and later by General Sir William Howe, who made the home his headquarters from which to direct the Battle of Germantown. In this historic home is a plaque, dedicated in honor of a black woman, with this inscription:

> *In memory of Dinah*
> *Faithful Colored caretaker of Stenton*
> *who by her quick thought and*
> *presence of mind saved the mansion*
> *from being burned by the British*
> *soldiers in the winter of 1777.*

BLACK ORGANIZATIONS, SOCIETIES AND SCHOOLS

Afro-American Insurance Company

The first known insurance firm to be owned and operated by blacks was the Afro-American Insurance Company, formed in Philadelphia in the early 1800s by Joseph Randolph, William Coleman, and James Porter. Its chief purpose was to provide persons of color with a Christian burial. Its original cash asset was $5000. The company had offices at 159 Lombard Street and 529 Lombard Street. It went out of business in 1840.

Banneker School

In 1789 a building which is considered the oldest school in Philadelphia, was erected to educate black children. Named for Benjamin Banneker, the name was later changed to the Harriet Beecher Stowe school for the famous author of *Uncle Tom's Cabin*, an antislavery novel written in 1852.

Benjamin Banneker was a self-taught black scientist and astronomer from the State of Maryland. He was a member of a commission surveying the District of Columbia. He was recommended to the commission by Thomas Jefferson. For several years Banneker published an almanac for the State of Pennsylvania, Delaware, Maryland and Virginia. He also wrote a letter to Jefferson questioning his contradictory views on slavery.

The Banneker Institute, a black literary society was founded in 1854, and located in Central Hall on Walnut Street above Sixth Street. Due to the policy of segregation at the seashore, the Institute felt a need to operate the Banneker House, a well-known resort for black people located a short distance from the beach at Cape May, New Jersey. Accommodations at the newly renovated house, in 1858, were six dollars per week for room and board.

Free School House

Certified by the Philadelphia Historical Commission as a building worthy of preservation, the two-story brick Free School House stands at 1223-25 Spring Street. It was built in 1831, at a cost of $2,520 by the Association of Friends for the instruction of poor black children.

The school operated sixty-six years before it was purchased by The Pennsylvania Abolition Society in 1908. The Society set up the Spring Street Settlement, a neighborhood work house for black boys and girls and a "Civil Center of Good Influence" for their people.

Institute for Colored Youth

In 1832 a Quaker named Richard Humphreys provided $10,000 in his will for a school for black youth. A farm was purchased on the outskirts of Philadelphia, and male youths comprised the first student body. Jonathan Zane, a sympathetic Quaker, willed $18,000 to the school. Shortly after the school opened a small rebellion took place and the school doors were closed. The students objected to the farm work and discipline and ran away from the school. The farm was sold and a new school was built in 1852 and called the Institute for Colored Youth. It was located on Lombard Street and designated as a high school. Its initial goal was to train teachers. The Institute enjoyed a good reputation, largely due to the efforts of Mrs. Fanny Jackson Coppin who served as principal from 1869 to 1900. Her successor, Mr. Hugh Browne, was instrumental in having the school removed from its city location in 1902 to Cheyney, Pennsylvania. It opened as a normal school in 1904, was later designated a state teachers college and today is called a state college.

The Philadelphia Library Company of Colored Persons

Instituted January 1, 1833, and incorporated in 1836, it was the most prominent literary and cultural organization of blacks in the state. The purpose of the Company, as its title implies, was the collection of a library of useful works of every description for the benefit of its members. Debating contests were frequently a part of the meeting. The Society was the first successful literary organization of its kind in the United States founded by blacks.

Existing during the same period as the Colored Library Company were the following black societies in Philadelphia:

Demostheian Institute, 1837
Edgeworth Society, 1837
Female Society, 1831
Gilbert Lyceum, 1841
Minerva Literary Association, 1834
Reading Room Society, 1828
Rush Library and Debating Society, 1836
Phyllis Wheatley Association, early 1900s

Another prominent black cultural organization founded on October 25, 1897, was the Afro-American Historical Society. The Society consisted of a dedicated group of men whose purpose was to preserve the black heritage.

Philadelphia Tribune

Christopher James Perry, Sr., founded the *Philadelphia Tribune*, the oldest continuously publishing black newspaper in the country. Born in Baltimore in 1836, Perry came to Philadelphia in 1873. He went to work for a Philadelphia daily paper writing a special column on social events and other black activities. In 1844, he published the first edition of the *Tribune* at 725 Sansom Street. Perry used the paper as a forum for his crusades for better jobs and better working conditions for blacks. The crusades urged black representation in the city government, and opposed discrimination, prejudice, and graft in politics. By 1912, it was necessary to move to bigger quarters. Perry then leased the present building at 526 South 16th Street.

Christopher Perry died in 1921.

Willing's Alley

The Free African School was located on Willing's Alley, a tiny street between Chestnut and Walnut and Third and Fourth Streets in Philadelphia's old financial district. It was controlled by the firm of Charles Willing and his son, Thomas, who both made fortunes in the slave trade. Their partner in these dealings was Robert Morris, who is immortalized as the father of American Banking. Later this building became the home of Anthony Benezet's school for black children.

The school house was a one-story brick building, approximately thirty-two feet by eighteen feet. Here Benezet also gave instructions to black adults in the evenings.

At the age of sixty-eight years, Benezet continued his volunteer services as a teacher. For years, the school was known as the Benezet School. When he died, Benezet left money to support the school.

CHURCHES

First African Presbyterian Church

In 1811 John Gloucester established, in Philadelphia, the First African Presbyterian Church. Gloucester's contribution to the Presbytery was highly significant because the appeal of this religious group to blacks was marginal since most Afro-Americans resisted their teaching.

Gloucester was the slave of Dr. Gideon Blackburn, a minister who came to Philadelphia from Tennessee. Impressed by Gloucester, Blackburn tutored him in religious thought and set him free to engage in missionary work.

In 1811 Gloucester and his congregation purchased a lot at 7th and Bainbridge Streets and built a church which became the First African Presbyterian Church. In 1882, the church was moved to the southeast corner of 16th and Lombard Streets. Seven years later it was moved to 17th and Fitzwater Streets. Today, the church is located at 42nd Street and Girard Avenue.

Mother Bethel

Mother Bethel (African Methodist Episcopal Church) is located on Sixth Street below Pine. The church occupies the oldest piece of ground in the United States continuously owned by black people.

Richard Allen started a school at the church and later taught other blacks to read and write. He became the church's first funeral director. In 1801 he published the first hymnal designed for the exclusive use by blacks, *A Collection of Hymns and Spiritual Songs from Various Authors*. The pulpit constructed and used by Allen is located in the church today.

Next to Allen, Bishop Daniel Payne was the greatest figure in the African Methodist Episcopal Church history. Payne served Mother Bethel from 1841 until 1844. As an educator, Payne mastered Greek, Latin, French, English and mathematics. He later served as president of Wilberforce University.

Old Christ Church

1695 saw the beginnings of a congregation for Old Christ's Church on Second Street, north of Market Street. The building on the present site began in 1727 and was completed in 1754 with the adding of the church tower and spire. The pews of

Benjamin Franklin, George Washington, Betsy Ross and Robert Morris are located in the church. Seven signers of the Declaration of Independence, including Benjamin Franklin, are buried in the church's burial ground.

The records of Christ Church show that blacks were baptized, married and served as members of the congregation as early as 1717. There was a minister who had special charge of the religious services for blacks.

St. Peter Claver's Catholic Church

Dedicated in 1892 as St. Peter Claver's Roman Catholic Church, this church was located at Twelfth and Lombard Streets for black Catholic parishioners. Until the purchase of this church, the black Catholics of the city had previously worshipped at St. Joseph's, St. Mary's and St. Augustine's. In 1886, mass was held for blacks at Holy Trinity Church at Sixth and Spruce Streets. During the 1920s, St. Peter Claver's permitted the various black literary and dramatic groups to perform and to conduct poetry contests within the church, thus contriving this grand tradition. The church was named in honor of Saint Peter Claver, who was born about 1518 (some historians say 1583) in the small principality of Catalonia in Spain. His humanitarian efforts towards emancipation of slaves was so great that he earned the title, "Apostle of the Slave Trade."

Zoar United Methodist Church

Located on Twelfth and Melon Streets, and founded in 1796, is the oldest established church among the Black Methodists in the area. The church was organized in a section known as Campingtown, Pennsylvania where soldiers camped. Its original name was the African Zoar Methodist Episcopal Church. The first church was an abandoned butcher shop located at Fourth and Brown Streets. The membership consisted of eighteen men and three women.

THE BUSINESS OF FOOD

Caterers Of Philadelphia

Peter Augustin was one of several prosperous and successful black caterers in Philadelphia. He came to the city from the West Indies and started his business in 1818. Many distinguished American and foreign guests were served at his restaurant located at 219 South Fifth Street.

From 1845 to 1875 the world of catering in Philadelphia was controlled by a group of black restaurateurs: Henry Jones, Thomas J. Dorsey, Henry Minton, and James Prosser. Dorsey was an escaped Maryland slave who later had his freedom purchased by friends in the city. He established his residence at 166 Locust Street and entertained noted members of the antislavery movement: William Lloyd Garrison, Charles Sumner, and Frederick Douglass. Dorsey and Henry Minton had an "undying reverence" for the abolitionists and contributed money to their cause.

P. Albert Dutrieville, born in Philadelphia in 1838, operated a successful establishment at 40 South Fifteenth Street. Dutrieville was the owner of the Caterers' Manufacturing and Supply Company and later served as the president of the Philadelphia Caterers Association.

During the mid-1800s James Prosser operated an oyster cellar which stood at 806 Market Street. However, the main labor of Prosser's little establishment was that of cooking terrapin, a North American fresh-water turtle, famous for its edible flesh. When Prosser died the business was taken over by his wife Sarah. Upon her death the business passed on to their son who later gave up the oyster cellar and became a caterer about 1875.

While traveling to Florence, Italy, Joseph W. Miller, a prominent Philadelphia citizen, wrote a poem entitled *Prosser's Journey to Heaven* or *The Triumph of Terrapin*. The poem describes Prosser seeking admission at the "Pearly Gates" of heaven. He informs Charon, the boatman, that the only payment he can give him is food. Charon accepts and Prosser is able to cross. The payment consists of "a dozen stewed" buckwheat cakes and Jersey sausage. Prosser is then met by the Furies whom he offers reed birds, softshell crabs, and Maurice River Coves. They too accept and finally he stands before St. Peter who asks for his ticket. He has no ticket but offers instead many specialties from his menu. None stirs the enthusiasm of St. Peter until he mentions terrapin. The verse begins:

> *"What! Stewed Terrapin, Jim Prosser!*
> *Open wide the gate are born—*
> *Here come Terrapin and Prosser!*
> *Make him welcome*
> *Peter shook his sides with laughter*
> *Stalked in Prosser, wildly gay:*
> *Lots of Terrapin came after—*
> *And our vision fled away."*

CRIES OF THE STREET VENDORS

The black street vendor has a long and interesting tradition in Philadelphia. A typical gathering place for these early vendors was the open market place at Head House Square. A re-creation of that market area is located at Second and Pine Streets.

After many years of absence, center city Philadelphia of the 70s has witnessed a profusion of black vendors. They are presently involved in a controversy, with store merchants, over their right to remain on the streets of Philadelphia.

"Hominy man come out to-day
For to sell his hominay
Hominy man is on his way,
for to sell his good hominay"

"Sea Bass!
Fine Sea-Bass!"

"Pepper-pot!
All hot! all hot!
Makee back strong!
Makee live long!
Come buy my Pepper pot!"

"Y'ere's the White Whitey-Wash!
Brown Whitey-Wash!
Yellow Whitey-Wash!
Green Whitey-Wash!
Wash, Wash!
I'm about!"

"Split wood!
Split wood!"

"Hot Corn!
Hot Corn!"

SLAVERY: MERCHANDISING AND MIGRATION

The London Coffee House

This historic tavern stood on the southwest corner of Front and High (now Market) Streets. In 1754, Major William Bradford, who was then publisher of the *Pennsylvania Journal* and grandson of the first Bradford who introduced printing to Pennsylvania, successfully established a coffee house after the London style. In the rear portion of the building, the *Pennsylvania Journal* was printed and sold. The front served as the meeting place of merchants, ship captains, judges, lawyers, city officials and Crown officers.

The Coffee House was originally built in 1702 by Charles Reed who obtained his lot from Laetitia Penn, the daughter of William Penn. The tavern operated as a coffee house because coffee was the main liquid consumed, although various types of liquor were also sold.

It was the common practice of the day to sell blacks at a public sale. At the old London Coffee House the slaves for sale were displayed upon a platform. Many other historical events took place at this corner and in the Coffee House. Included among these were the Stamp Act papers, and the Royal Arms which were publicly burned here after the reading of the Declaration of Independence by John Nixon.

Once located in a section of the city near Water and Market Streets was the Old Slave Market. Prospective buyers came there often to examine and to purchase the cargo of newly arrived slaves during Colonial Philadelphia times.

Robert Morris House

Robert Morris and Benjamin Franklin did more than any other individuals to help finance the Revolution. The commercial firm of Morris and Willing, from 1754 to 1766, brought hundreds of blacks from Africa and sold them into slavery. When the Pennsylvania legislature voted to ban further importation from Africa, it was declared that only the wealthy, including Morris and Willing, profited from the trade. Thomas Willing, the son, participated in the trade upon his father's death. In 1761, the firm of Willing and Morris advertised for the sale of a hundred and seventy blacks who had just arrived from the Gold Coast of Africa. Morris was later confined to debtor's prison.

Another eminent slave merchant was Joseph Turner who became one of the trustees of what is now the University of Pennsylvania. Among the leading colonial slave dealers was the prominent Philadelphia Quaker, Isaac Norris II, for whose father the Montgomery County seat of Norristown, Pennsylvania is named.

Runaway Slave Newspaper Advertisements

Blacks who were enslaved were constantly and understandably seeking freedom by running away from their masters. *The American Weekly Mercury*, the first newspaper printed in Philadelphia in the year 1719, advertised in its second issue that a bright mulatto by the name of Johnny had run away. The sale of black women slaves frequently appeared in this newspaper.

Following are some ads as they appeared:

FOR SALE FEMALE SLAVE

A very likely Negro woman to be sold, aged about 28 years. Fit for country or city business. She can card, spin, knit and milk; and any other country work. Whoever has a mind for the said Negro report to Andrew Bradford in Philadelphia.

Run away on the 4th Instant, at night from James Leonard in Middlesex County, East-New Jersey, a Negro man named Simon, aged 40 years, is well-set fellow, about 5 feet 10 inches high, has large Eyes, and a foot 12 inches long; he was bred and born in this Country, talks good English, can read and write, is very slow in speech, can Bleed and Draw Teeth Pretending to be a Great Doctor and very Religious, and says he is a Churchman, had on a dark grey Broadcloth Coat, with a good apparel, and peeked toe'd shoes. He took with him a Black Horse, about 13 hands and a half-high, a Star in forehead, branded with 2 on the near Thigh or Shoulder, and trots; also a black hunting saddle about half worn. Whoever takes up and secures the said Negro, so that his Master may have him again shall have three pounds reward and reasonable charges, paid by James Leonard.
Sept. 11, 1740

Run away on the 16th of July from Thomas Rutter, of this city a Negro Man, named Dick, commonly called Preaching Dick, aged about 27 years.
Thomas Rutter
Sept. 4, 1746

No Ads For Slaves

Formerly the home of Christopher Sower or Sauer, an American printer born in Germany in 1693, the house at 5300 Germantown Avenue now belongs to the Trinity Lutheran Church. Sower introduced the first type to America imported from Germany, printed the first book in German in America and the first German newspaper in 1739. In 1743 he printed a German bible, the second bible printed in this country, the first having been the bible translated into the *Indian Language*. Christopher Sower consistently refused to accept advertisements for sales or for runaway slaves. Benjamin Franklin carried these advertisements during the early days of his *Pennsylvania Gazette*. Franklin later discontinued the practice of slave advertisement.

Antislavery Fairs

In the city of Philadelphia, from 1835 to 1861, women abolitionists organized annual fairs to benefit the Philadelphia Female Anti-Slavery Society. The fairs were held at a number of public halls and private estates throughout the city, and a great variety of articles were offered for sale—fruits and nuts, ice cream, pies, lemonades, and jellies were among the delicacies. Though similar fairs were being organized in other states, the Philadelphia fair was the largest and was known internationally, with goods being sent from other countries such as England, France and Germany.

The fairs also were occasions to publicize the cause of antislavery and honor its heroes, who were invited to speak at them. Two black leaders were among the celebrated speakers in 1859—the wealthy Philadelphia abolitionist Robert Purvis and William Wells Brown, author of the first black play, and the first black novel written in 1852. Brown's novel *Clotel* or, *The President's Daughter* is based on Thomas Jefferson's alleged slave daughter.

In his autobiography, *Memoirs of the Author* which appears in his book *The Black Man*, written in 1863, Brown writes: "I was born at Lexington, Kentucky. My father, as I was informed, was a member of the Wickliffe family, my mother was of mixed blood; her father it was said, was the noted Daniel Boone, and her mother a Negress." Boone was born in Berks County, Pennsylvania. The Boone Homestead and Museum is located a mile north of U.S. 422 at Baumstown.

Frances Ellen Harper, one of the best-known black antislavery poets of her day, participated in several of these fairs.

It is generally accepted that this Philadelphia poet became the first black woman to write a novel. *Iola LeRoy, or Shadows Uplifted*, published in Boston in 1892.

There exists evidence that Emma Kelley may have been the first black woman to publish a novel. (See the Introduction for discussion of Emma Kelley.)

Female Anti-Slavery Society

Organized in Philadelphia on December 9, 1833, by the Quaker woman abolitionist Lucretia Mott, the office of the Society was located at National Hall on Market Street. The Society consisted of sixty women, both white and black. Among the black members were the daughters of wealthy abolitionist James Forten; Sarah, Harriet, and Margarette, who conducted a private school for black students along with Sarah Douglass. Although Sarah was born a Quaker, she later refused to attend meetings because a special bench was designated for blacks. The Society's main function was to help in the elimination of slavery. Its influence was so profound that similar societies were organized throughout the eastern seaboard. The Society existed until after the Civil War, then occupying itself with the fate of the black freedman. Lucretia Mott focused her attention on the liberation of women until her death when the *Philadelphia Record* for Friday, November 12, 1880, carried an article on its front page which read:

Lucretia Mott Dead
Philadelphia's Most Distinguished Woman Passed
Away. A Life Spent in the Cause of Liberty, Humanity
and the Advancement of Women

The Pennsylvania Abolition Society

On April 14, 1775, a meeting of Quakers and other religious groups took place at Sun Tavern on Second Street in Philadelphia to organize this country's oldest and most honored abolition society. For a number of years various religious groups released their personal slaves from bondage as a matter of conscience. However, once freed many of these blacks were kidnapped and sold back into slavery. The abolitionists realized that if their freeing of the slaves was to be truly effective, legal advice had to be provided to the freed people. The individuals meeting at Sun Tavern decided to try to fill this need, and that night they organized *The Society for the Relief of Free Negroes, Unlawfully Held in Bondage*.

The Society was an effective action group. Among its members were some of the most prominent men of the times—Benjamin Franklin, Tom Paine, Benjamin Rush, and the Marquis de Lafayette. As the organization grew, its members realized that its original purpose was too limited. While the relief of free blacks was still needed, a greater goal was desired. In 1787, the Society adopted a new constitution and along with it a new name: *The Pennsylvania Society for Promoting the Abolition of Slavery: The Relief of Free Negroes Unlawfully Held in Bondage; and for Improving the Condition of the African Race*.

The Abolition Society exists today to provide educational and informational services.

The American Colonization Society

The American Colonization Society, founded as an alliance of missionaries and southern slaveholders, came into being as the result of thoughtful consideration of the blacks, both free and slave. The society was organized in 1816 in Washington, D.C.; its purpose was to find a satisfactory solution to the black problem by enforced emigration to Africa. Francis Scott Key, the author of the *Star Spangled Banner*, considered a friend of the blacks, was one of the founders of the society. When Jesse Torrey, Jr., a Philadelphia physician, attempted to aid a group of free blacks who had been kidnapped and placed in slavery, Key volunteered his legal services without charge.

The Colonization Society received strong support from prominent slaveowners. The Colonization Society's solution was to transport the blacks to Sherbo Island and Liberia, Africa.

The Colonization Society encountered difficulties in establishing a permanent settlement on Sherbo Island. Many of the transplanted American blacks became ill and died. However, the settlement of Liberia struggled on and survived.

Blacks in several states immediately recognized this scheme as a plan to get rid of free blacks and to make the institution of slavery more secure. The free blacks in Pennsylvania and their white allies formed a state council to attack the hypocrisy of the American Colonization Society. The integrated body chose for its name the Anti-Colonization Society and Women's Rights Ticket.

FOOTNOTES

California House Riot–Once standing at the northwest corners of St. Mary and Sixth Streets, the house was named in honor of the newest addition to the Union, California. The property was occupied by a black man who was married to a white woman. On October 9, 1849, a group of whites from Moyamensing planned to attack the *California House*. The group, resenting the marriage of the proprietors of the house, vowed to burn it to the ground. However, the black residents of St. Mary's Street heard of the planned attack and prepared themselves for the defense of their neighborhood from the whites.

A riot began as the group from Moyamensing entered the *California House*. The group destroyed the barroom, breaking the fixtures and furniture, piled them in the middle of the floor and set them on fire. The unarmed city police who came to prevent further violence between the races met revolving pistols, knives, and clubs, and were driven back toward Lombard Street. The crowd held in check the Hope Fire Company and the Good Will Fire Company who arrived on the scene. Charles Himmelwright, a member of the Good Will Fire Company, was shot and killed, while John Hollick died after being wounded.

Girard College–Stephen Girard, a Frenchman by birth, lived in Philadelphia and through successful trade in the West Indies became one of the richest Americans of his time. At his death in 1831 he bequeathed a large sum of money toward establishment of Girard College, on nearly forty acres of land bordering Girard Avenue in North Philadelphia. The stipulations in his will—that the College be for "poor white boys" only, and that a high wall be built around it—sparked one of the longest cases in Philadelphia legal history. Even though the College is situated in the midst of Philadelphia's black community, the city adhered to the stipulation for a hundred years until a noted black lawyer, Raymond Pace Alexander, the first black judge to serve on the Philadelphia Common Pleas Court, charged the city with discrimination. He opened the legal challenge in the 1930s; it was not won until the mid- 1960s when, under the auspices of another skillful black lawyer, Cecil B. Moore, the United States Supreme Court decided against the legality of Girard's will.

There appears to be some confusion about controversial Stephen Girard, his wealth and how he came about the large accumulation. Joel A. Rogers in *100 Amazing Facts About the Negro* reports that Toussaint L'Ouverture saved 6,000,000 gold francs which he entrusted to Stephen Girard, then an American captain, for safekeeping. L'Ouverture planned to make Dahomey in West Africa his base for fighting slave trade after freeing Haiti. After Toussaint's capture, Girard would not return his money.

Another view of Girard's story suggests that Girard received valuables placed in his care on board his vessels that were never claimed because the owners were destroyed in the fighting, by rebellious blacks. Evidence to prove this is unreliable.

In addition to money willed for Girard College, he bequeathed freedom and two hundred dollars a year to his black female servant Hannah.

Agrippa Hull–The house standing on the corner of Third and Pine Streets in Philadelphia was once the home of Revolutionary War General Thaddeus Kosciuszko who, from the time of his arrival in America in 1777, took an interest in the plight of the black man. Agrippa Hull, a free black man from Northampton, Massachusetts served under the General, and before the Polish General, Hull served as a private for General John Paterson of the Massachusetts Line. Returning to Stockbridge, Massachusetts after the war, he married a fugitive slave and adopted a daughter, also a fugitive. There was an affectionate reunion when Kosciuszko returned to visit the U.S. and Hull traveled to New York to see him. On this visit Kosciuszko was awarded a gift of land in Ohio. He directed that it be sold to found a school for blacks.

The celebrated Polish General authorized Thomas Jefferson to dispose of his property. Jefferson, being of old age, instructed an attorney, Benjamin Lincoln Lear of New Jersey, to execute the Pole's will. In spite of continuous legal battles the school never became a reality.

The Lantern Holder–Black historian Earl Koger recently revealed that, historically, the lantern holder figurine symbolized a twelve year old black boy named Jocko who held a group of horses near Trenton, New Jersey, as George Washington's army crossed the Delaware River on December 24, 1776. Jocko was frozen to death performing this service. Impressed by this young man, George Washington had a statue erected on his lawn at Mount Vernon honoring Jocko. Replicas of the Jocko statue have changed over the years.

Prior to the Civil War, it was the custom of some Abolitionists to place small figurines holding lanterns on their property to alert fugitives that their home was a station on the Underground Railroad.

The Library Company of Philadelphia and Historical Society of Pennsylvania–Established in 1731 by Benjamin Franklin as the first lending library in the United States, The Library Company at 1314 Locust Street has one of the largest and finest archives on the American blacks from the 1600s to the early 1900s. In 1969 the two venerable institutions jointly held an exhibition, the first major exhibition of its kind in America. *Negro History: 1553-1903*. It consisted of prints, books, black made paintings, and manuscripts. The emphasis of the exhibition was on contributions of blacks to their own history. In April of 1974, the Historical Society of Pennsylvania staged a significant exhibition, the celebration of the Pennsylvania Abolition Society. The exhibition was titled *The Pennsylvania Abolition Society and the Pennsylvania Black*. Among the items shown in this exhibition was Charles Willson Peale's painting of *Yarrow Mamout*

who served as a spy for George Washington. Mamout became well known and drew the attention of Peale, who saw in the face of this old Mooi a legion of experience. Mamout refused to use his slave name, he identified himself with his African ancestry. The painting can be viewed at the Historical Society of Pennsylvania. One of the black treasures displayed on the walls at the Library Company is Samuel Jenning's large painting of *Liberty Displaying the Arts and Science*. The painting depicts a group of blacks representing freedom from captivity. The Library Company proudly displays a bust of the first huge statue of liberty, the *Goddess Minerva as the Patroness of American Liberty*.

Mikveh Cemetery, Lucy Mark Grave–A slave of the prominent Jewish Mark family of Philadelphia, Lucy Mark took her master's surname, as was the common practice during the period of slavery. According to historian Maxwell Whiteman, Lucy was a member of the congregation Mikveh Israel in the 1790s, and also a member of the ladies of Mikveh Israel, observing the traditions of Judaism.

Upon her death in 1823, the family applied for the customary burial in the historic synagogue's cemetery, located on Spruce Street. Some of the affluent members of the congregation protested the burial of a servant in the synagogue's cemetery. After a short delay and intense support from other members, Lucy was buried in an unmarked grave near the entrance of the cemetery. Rebecca Gratz, in attempting to have her non-Jewish mother buried in the same cemetery used the fact of Lucy Mark's grave to illustrate that the cemetery had already received non-Jews and this privilege should be extended to her parent. Rebecca Gratz was unsuccessful in changing the rules of Mikveh Israel's cemetery.

The Mummer's Parade–Originating in England in the early 1800s, the Mummers' Parade has been, for years, a traditional part of Philadelphia's folklore. Dressed in a variety of highly decorated costumes, participants representing numerous clubs and organizations compete for prizes offered by the city and various civic and business associations, by marching down Broad Street. Adding to this joyous celebration before thousands of spectators is the music of string bands and the performances of comic divisions.

During the early 1960s, groups portraying black-face minstrel characters were viewed as stereotypes by the protesting black citizens of Philadelphia. Consequently, due to the pressure placed upon the organizers of the Mummer's Parade, the practice was eliminated.

Traditionally a father/son organization born out of South Philadelphia, no women participated until 1975. The parade is customarily held on New Year's Day on Broad Street in Philadelphia. The theme song heard from the many string bands is black composer James Bland's *Oh, Dem Golden Slippers*. The performers appear to be imitating early Negro dancers in such characteristic "cakewalk" figures. No blacks perform in the Mummers' Parade.

The Union League–Occupying one city block, with an entrance located on Broad Street, the Union League Club was formed after military defeats and Republican election losses of 1862 in Philadelphia and other northern cities.

The function of the early organization was to distribute war literature and to raise money for soldier relief. The Union League of Philadelphia played a vital role in recruiting black volunteers during the Civil War. The League participated in the organization of Camp William Penn, the all black camp located at what is now La Mott, Pennsylvania, a few miles north of the city. After the war, the League aided the officials of the Freedmen's Bureau in developing a strong Republican political organization to elect black legislators in the South. The noted black educator and founder of Tuskegee Institute, Booker T. Washington, was invited to deliver a lecture at the League in Philadelphia on February 12, 1899, but a snow storm prevented his train arrival on that day. He accommodated the Union League at a public reception the next day at a member's residence.

The Union League today has survived as a predominantly white conservative organization.

BIBLIOGRAPHY

APTHEKER, HERBERT, *The Negro in the American Revolution,* International Publishers, New York, 1940.

BARKSDALE, RICHARD AND KINNAMON, KENNETH, *Black Writers of America: A Comprehensive Anthology,* The MacMillan Co., New York, 1972.

BARNES, GILBERT, *The Anti-Slavery Impulse,* The American Historical Association, New York, 1933.

BEDINI, SILVIO A., *The Life of Benjamin Banneker,* Charles Scribner's Sons, 1972.

BELL, HOWARD H., "National Negro Conventions of the Middle 1840's: Moral Suasion Vs. Political Action" *Journal of Negro History,* XLII (October, 1957), 147-260.

BELL, WHITFIELD J., JR., "Washington County Pennsylvania, in the Eighteenth Century Anti-Slavery Movement" *Western Pennsylvania Historical Magazine,* XXV (September, December 1942), 125-142.

BENNETT, LERONE, JR., *Pioneers in Protest,* Johnson Publishing Co., Inc. Chicago, 1968.

BILLINGTON, RAY ALLAN, "James Forten: Forgotten Abolitionist" *Negro History Bulletin,* XIII (November, 1949), 31-36-45.

BLESH, JUDY AND HARRIET, JANIS, *They All Played Ragtime,* Grove Press Inc., 1950.

BLOCKSON, CHARLES L., "The History of the Black Man in Montgomery County" *The Bulletin of the Historical Society of Montgomery County,* XVIII (No. 4, 1973), 337-362.

BROOKES, GEORGE S., *Friend Anthony Benezet,* Oxford University Press, Philadelphia, 1934.

BROWN, IRA V., "The Negro in Pennsylvania History" *The Pennsylvania History Studies,* The Pennsylvania Historical Association (No. 11, 1970).

CATTO, REV. WILLIAM T., "A Semi Centenary Discourse," Delivered in the First African Presbyterian Church, Philadelphia, 1857.

CHILD, MARIA L., *The Freedmen's Book*, Ticknor and Fields, Boston, 1865.

DAVIS, ARTHUR P., *From the Dark Tower*, Howard University Press, 1974.

DAVIS, ARTHUR P., and REDDING, SAUNDERS, *Cavalcade*, Houghton Mifflin Co., 1971.

DAVIS, GEORGE, "Pittsburgh—Negro Troops in the Civil War" *Western Pennsylvania Historical Magazine*, XXXVI (June, 1953).

DAVIS, W. W. H., "Negro Slavery in Bucks County," *The History of Bucks County*, Doylestown, 1876, 793-803.

DAYTON, H., *Fifty Years in Chains: or, The Life of an American Slave*, J. J. Read, New York, 1858.

D'ELIA, DONALD J., "Dr. Benjamin Rush and the Negro," *Journal of Negro History of Ideas*, XXX (July-September, 1969), 413-422.

DOVER, CEDRIC, *American Negro Art*, New York Graphic Art Library, 1960.

DUBOIS, W. E. B., *The Philadelphia Negro: A Social Study, Philadelphia*, Published for the University of Pennsylvania, Ginn & Co., Boston, 1899.

DUMOND, DWIGHT L., *Antislavery: The Crusade for Freedom in America*, University of Michigan Press, 1961.

Ethnic Studies in Lawrence County—Negroes, Published by the Pennsylvania Historical and Museum Commission in 1939 as a WPA project.

GIBSON, RUFUS, "The Negro in Pennsylvania," *Negro History Bulletin*, V (December, 1941), 52-58.

GREENE, LORENZO J., "The Negro in the War of 1818 and the Civil War", *Negro History Bulletin*, XIV (March, 1951), 133-137.

GUTHRIE, CHAPLIN, JAS. M., *Camp-Fires of the Afro-American or the Colored Man as a Patriot*, Afro American Publishing Co., Philadelphia, 1899.

HARTGROVE, W. B., "The Negro Soldier in the American Revolution", *Journal of Negro History*, I:2 (April, 1916), 110-131.

HENSEL, W. U., *The Christiana Riot and the Treason Trials of 1851*, the New Era Printing Co., Lancaster, 1911.

HORNBACK, FLORENCE M., "Survey of the Negro Population of Johnstown, Pennsylvania", *Johnstown Tribune*, 1941.

JACKSON, JOSEPH, *Encyclopedia of Philadelphia*, National History Association, Harrisburg, 1932.

KAPLAN, SIDNEY, *The Black Presence in the Era of the American Revolution: 1770-1800*, New York Graphic Society Ltd. in association with the Smithsonian Institution Press, 1973.

KATZ, WILLIAM LOREN, *The Black West,* Doubleday, 1971.

KOEHLER, LEROY, *The History of Monroe County, Pennsylvania, During the Civil War,* Historical Society of Monroe County, 1950.

LEE, JARENA, *Religious Experience and Journal of . . . Giving an Account of Her Call to Preach the Gospel, Revised and Corrected from the Original Manuscript written by Herself,* Philadelphia, 1849.

"Letters of Dr. F. Julius Le Moyne, An Abolitionist of Western Pennsylvania", *Journal of Negro History,* XVIII (October, 1933), 451-474.

The Liberty Bell, By Friends of Freedom, Boston, 1839.

LIVERMORE, GEORGE, *An Historical Research Respecting: The Opinions of the Founders of the Republic on Negroes As Slaves, As Citizens, and As Soldiers,* A. Williams and Co., Boston, 1863.

McCLURE, ALEXANDER K., *Old-Time Notes of Pennsylvania,* 2 vols., Philadelphia, 1905.

MAZYCK, WALTER M., *George Washington and the Negro,* The Associated Publishers, Inc., Washington, 1932.

"*Memorial of the Free Citizens of Color in Pittsburgh and its Vicinity, Relative to the Rights of Suffrage*", Harrisburg, 1837.

MILLER, KELLY, "The Historical Background of the Negro Physician", *Journal of Negro History,* I (April, 1916), 99-109.

"*Minutes of the State Convention of the Colored Citizens of Pennsylvania*", Convened at Harrisburg, December 13th and 14th, 1848.

MOTT, A., *Biographical Sketches and Interesting Anecdotes of Persons of Color,* New York, 1837.

MURRAY, LINDLEY, *Narratives of Colored Americans,* New York, 1882.

MYER, A. C., ed., *Narrative of Early Pennsylvania, West New Jersey and Delaware,* 1860.

Narrative of Henry Box Brown, Who Escaped from Slavery Enclosed in a Box Three Feet Long and Two Feet Wide, Boston, 1849.

Narrative of the Proceedings of the Black People, During the Late and Awful Calamity in Philadelphia, in the Year 1793: and A Refutation of some Censures, Thrown Upon Them in Some late Publications, Absalom Jones and Richard Allen, Philadelphia, 1794.

NASH, GARY B., "Slave and Slave Owners in Colonial Philadelphia", *William Quarterly* (April, 1973), 223-256.

NELL, WILLIAM C., *The Colored Patriot of the American Revolution,* Boston, 1855.

OBLINGER, CARL D., *Freedoms Foundations: Black Communities in Southeastern Pennsylvania Towns: 1780-1860,* Northwest and Missouri State University, 1972.

PENN, I. GARLAND, *The Afro-American Press and Its Editors,* Springfield, Mass., 1891.

Pennsylvania–A Guide to the Keystone State, Compiled by the Writer's Program of the Work Projects' Administration in the State of Pennsylvania, New York, 1940.

PORTER, DOROTHY B., "The Organized Educational Activities of Negro Literary Societies: 1828-1846", *Journal of Negro Education,* V (October, 1936), 555-576.

PORTER, DOROTHY B., *Early Negro Writing: 1760-1837,* Beacon Press, Boston, 1971.

PORTER, JAMES A., *Modern Negro Art,* Dryden Press, New York, 1943.

POWELL, JOHN M., *Bring Out Your Dead: The Great Plague of Yellow Fever in Philadelphia in 1793,* Philadelphia, 1949.

Proceedings of the State Equal Rights, Convention of the Colored People of Pennsylvania held in the City of Harrisburg, February 8th, 10th, and 19th, 1865, Harrisburg, 1865.

PURVIS, ROBERT, *Appeal of Forty Thousand Colored Citizens, Threatened with Disenfranchisement, to The People of Pennsylvania,* Philadelphia, 1838.

QUARLES, BENJAMIN, *The Negro in the American Revolution,* University of North Carolina Press, 1961.

QUARLES, BENJAMIN, *Black Abolitionists,* Oxford University Press, 1969.

ROGERS, J. A., *Africa's Gift to America,* Futuro Press, Inc., New York, 1959.

ROLLIN, FRANK A., *Life and Public Services of Martin R. Delany,* Lee and Shepard Co., Boston, 1868.

ROSENBERGER, LYLE L., "Black Suffrage in Bucks County: The Election of 1837", *Bucks County Historical Society Journal,* (Spring, 1974).

ROSENBERGER, HOMER T., "Montgomery County's Greatest lady: Lucretia Mott", *The Bulletin of the Historical Society of Montgomery County,* VI (April, 1948), 91-171.

RUSSELL, ADAMS, *Great Negroes Past and Present,* Afro-American Publishing Co., 1963.

SILLEN, SAMUEL, *Women Against Slavery,* Masses and Mainstream, New York, 1955.

SIMMONS, WILLIAM J., *Men of Mark: Eminent, Progressive and Rising,* W. W. Williams Co., Cleveland, 1887.

SOUTHERN, EILEEN, *The Music of Black Americans: A History,* W. W. Norton and Co., New York, 1971.

STERLING, DOROTHY, *Speak Out in Thunder Tones: Letters and Other Writings by Black Northerners: 1787-1865*, Doubleday and Co., New York, 1973.

STILL, WILLIAM, *A Brief Narrative of the Struggle for the Rights of the Colored People of Philadelphia in the City Railway Cars*, Philadelphia, 1867.

TROTTER, JAMES M., *Music and Some Musical People*, Lee and Shepard Publishers, New York, 1878.

TURNER, EDWARD R., "The Abolition of Slavery in Pennsylvania", *Pennsylvania Magazine of History and Biography*, XXXVI (912), 129-142.

"The Negro in Pennsylvania: Slavery-Servitude-Freedom, 1639-1861", Washington, 1911.

"Slavery in Colonial Pennsylvania", *Pennsylvania Magazine of History and Biography*, XXXV (1911), 141-151.

WALKER, JOSEPH E., "Negro Labor in the Charcoal Iron Industry of Southeastern Pennsylvania", *Pennsylvania Magazine of History and Biography*, XCIII (October, 1969), 466-486.

WESLEY, CHARLES H., *Richard Allen: Apostle of Freedom*, The Associated Publishers, Inc., Washington, 1935.

WHITEMAN, MAXWELL, ed., *Afro-American History Series*, Historic Publications, Philadelphia, 1970.

WHITEMAN, MAXWELL, *The Kidnapped and the Ransomed*, The Narrative of Peter and Vina Still After Forty Years of Slavery with an Introductory Essay on Jews in the Antislavery Movement, Jewish Publication Society, Philadelphia, 1970.

WILLIAMS, GEORGE WASHINGTON, *History of the Negro Race in America from 1619 to 1880*, 2 vols, G. P. Putnam's Sons, New York, 1883.

WILLIAMS, KENNY J., *They Also Spoke: An Essay on Negro Literature in America: 1787-1930*, Townsend Press, Nashville, 1970.

WILLSON, JOSEPH, *Sketches of the Higher Classes of Colored Society in Philadelphia*, 1841.

WOLF, EDWIN, 2nd, *Negro History: 1553-1903*, Library Company of Philadelphia, 1969.

WOODSON, CARTER G., "The Negro in Pennsylvania", *Negro History Bulletin*, XII (1949), 150-152-167.

WRIGHT, RICHARD R., JR., *The Negro in Pennsylvania: A Study in Economic History*, Philadelphia, 1922.

YERKES, HARMON, "Anti-Slavery Days—Experiences of Fugitives", *Bucks County Historical Society Papers*, III (1909), 504-512.

INDEX